Voice of Death

Voice of Death

Traditional Thought and Modern Science

edited by
Baidyanath Saraswati

D.K. Printworld (P) Ltd.
New Delhi

N.K. Bose Memorial Foundation
Varanasi

Cataloging in Publication Data — DK
[Courtesy: D.K. Agencies (P) Ltd. <docinfo@dkagencies.com>]

Voice of death : traditional thought and modern science / edited by Baidyanath Saraswati.
vi, 226 p. 23 cm.
Includes passages in Sanskrit (Devanagari and roman)
Papers presented at a conference on the theme: Death in traditional thought and modern science.
Includes bibliographical references.
Includes index.
Contents: pt. 1. Philosophy and religion — pt. 2. Science and society.
ISBN 8124602743

1. Death — Congresses. 2. Death — Religious aspects — Congresses. 3. Philosophy and science — India — Congresses. I. Saraswati, Baidyanath, 1932 –

DDC 179.7 21

ISBN 81-246-0274-3
First Published in India in 2005

Published by:
D.K. Printworld (P) Ltd.
Regd. office : *'Sri Kunj'*, F-52, Bali Nagar, New Delhi - 110 015
Phones : (011) 2545-3975; 2546-6019; *Fax* : (011) 2546-5926
E-mail : dkprintworld@vsnl.net *Web* : www.dkprintworld.com

and

N.K. Bose Memorial Foundation
B, 8/9, Bara Gambhir Singh, Varanasi - 221001 (UP)
Phone : (0542) 2275289; *E-mail* : nkbfoundation@yahoo.com

Printed by: D.K. Printworld (P) Ltd., New Delhi.

Contents

PART II
SCIENCE AND SOCIETY

Introduction

Baidyanath Saraswati

FROM the viewpoint of anthropology the acceptance of a theory depends greatly upon its fitness to holistic perspective. This is what Nirmal Kumar Bose used to say. As an illustration to this pragmatism, a conference was organized on his thirtieth death anniversary. The theme was "Death in Traditional Thought and Modern Science." The participants were indologists, anthropologists, sociologists, philosophers and physical and social scientists, with a view that this venture may serve as a support in leading a desirable world-view and a valid theory of death.

Theme

Life and death are universal. But do they stand at the same level? Or is there a principle of life on the one hand and a principle of death on the other? Did they start off together or sequencely one after another. With whom do they continue? How do they unfold themselves in the world of the living? Do they belong to the same order of reality as that of the sky? Are they involved in maintaining the cosmic process? Is there a third entity beyond life and death? Can man ever find a key to this universal reality? By knowing death can one reach to a state of deathlessness? What is that state? Is it an existential state of mankind alone? Or does it apply to all creatures? Will there be the end of the world? Can one think of immortality within the world of life and death? Well, if the change of body is the play of the Soul, how about the theory of evolution which is vague and unpredictable?

Traditional cultures, haunted by the problem of death, have raised such questions and found answers in their own wisdom. According to the Hindu scriptures, death is not the sequel of sin or evil but the very condition of authentic life. Death is suffused in light. Immortality is reached only through death. No one becomes immortal with the body. Death is not evil. It leads man to the world of God and God to the world of man. There is a world of ancestors (*pitṛloka*). This reflects cosmic solidarity, the two-fold reality. Death is the end of an earthly road as also the gateway to the sky, making the whole universe a unity. It may also be viewed as the one that stands for cosmic transformation, signifying continual resurrection to a new life. Buddhism and Jainism correspond to this wisdom-view of death. The Vedic, Upaniṣadic and Paurāṇic thoughts are not hard to find among followers of Buddhist and Jain traditions.

Judaism, Christianity and Islam have also found answers to the mystery of death. Death is truly overcome when it is seen in God himself. This thought lies at the heart of the mystery of God's incarnation and His suffering and death. He was resurrected for man's sins and salvation. Judeo-Christianity and Islam hold in common the presence of God in human time. Hinduism recognizes the incarnation of God in human and animal forms. All these religions have dealt with, at great length, the concept of body, soul and the one or more than one heavenly God, identified as the transcendental and universal truth.

Aboriginal cultures view afterlife as something basically similar to the life on earth. They do not conceive of heaven as more beautiful than earth. Death is no different than other life transitions. The only differences that can be pointed out is that in death continuity is maintained not by the ever-changing physical body but by the spirit. In most initiatic societies there are archetypal phases in life when a person changes at each major juncture. In this world-view one has to accept the adventure of continual death and rebirth. It can be grasped only in terms of spiritual principles. Death is the constant companion of the living. The importance of Death-ritual is widely accepted. The "afterlife" refers to the anthropocosmic unity taken as reality.

Modern man concentrates on life and tends to wipe out all dealings with the dying and the dead. This attitude is fundamentally different from the traditional thought where both birth and death are held as occasions for celebration. Modernity aims at transcending the temporal order and conquering the sky. Will such a venture be possible at any point of time? What is "real" immortal life? Does immortality mean clinging to body? If so, it cannot be the "life" artificially alive as in modern hospitals.

Death is something larger than life. In Hindu religious context it is named as Śiva, the "auspicious one," the God of Death and dissolution. He is Mahākāla, the Great time, the absolute principle, the universal causality. He has a "third eye" that destroys the world. The Chinese word *shih* refers to time in general, indicating qualitative duration. Time is thought of as a union of "vital principles" (*ch'i*) producing life. Time and 'beginning' begin and end together: when a being disappears he ends, and with him his time, too, ends.

Scientists have raised questions: Why some species die out and others continue? Were they inferior organisms? Bad genes? Is it the law of nature (genetics) or nurture (environment)? Species change gradually into new species. The ancestral species does not die; it merely gets transformed into another species. Why some species live longer and others (humans) have a limited life-span? Why a species could not live for ever? Is extinction important? Traditional cultures take a cosmic view. Some (holy) places as well as (sacred) time provide *mokṣa* (earthly extinction) to pious individuals (men, animals and birds). The view of death in the sacred science seems to be different from that of the view of the modern science. "Is it true?"

Voices

The voices create a climate of opinion. Reason and logic cry out in pain, but mankind has learnt not to bother too much with reason and logic. The faith determines the course of life, but at certain moments it ceases to have determinable positions. It often finds a way of moving up in two orbits. Or cling to what appears to be the substantial world, as defined in philosophy, religion, science and social life.

PHILOSOPHY AND RELIGION

The dictionary definition of philosophy reads: "the rational investigation of being, knowledge and right conduct." The Sanskrit word for philosophy is *darśana* (sight), that is, "great thinking" or talking about what is "seen" and what is "unseen"? Grammatically, the English word "religion" comes from *re-legrere*, i.e., "gather," "collect." Philosophically it tends towards *re-ligare*, i.e., what unites, links up man to his divinity. The Sanskrit word *dharma* (Pāli, *dhamma*) is far more comprehensive than "religion." Derived from *dhṛ* (to hold, keep, maintain) it reflects in different contexts, such as attributes of mind, functions of the sense-organs, duty, nature of attributes, etc.

The voice of death raised in philosophy and religion creates a climate of faith. Scriptures sanctify faith and point out that our universe consists of both matter and spirit. The body is made up of matter; what lives in the body is soul. This is the "theory of theories" of life and death. A theory which delivers an inward grace is regarded as religion.

The views by R.C. Sharma deal with the Upaniṣadic concept of death: Death is not a fearful or a horrifying event. It is an essential phase of life and has to be accepted as such, on occasions. The ancient sages had expressed joyous feeling even at the time of death. They were quite friendly with the God of Death (Yama) and no iota of fear penetrated into their mind. *Death is not the extinction of life,* it opens a horizon for new journey on this planet or the other. With the passage of time the horrifying picture of hell and the presiding God of Death appeared.

Bettina Bäumer takes up the *Īśa Upaniṣad* to enlighten further. Death is an encounter with light. The dying person identifies himself with the glory, radiance and energy which signify the essence of light. The realization of one's true being takes place at the moment of death. This is the discovery of one's identity with the divine person (*Puruṣa*) whose vision is most glorious, beautiful and saving. Once this ultimate experience takes place, what remains of a person is the body which returns to the earth-element in the form of ashes, and his breath merges in the universal and immortal wind.

K.N. Sahay seeks connection between philosophy and religion and offers a comprehensive account of death as perceived in scriptures and religious traditions. For the primitives death is a wonder. What happens after death? How does the soul leave the body? Where does it go? The anthropologist, Sahay, confronts all such fundamental questions and tells us that the form of the soul can be photographed, a subject which has developed in Europe and called *ectoplasm*, a substance which contains finer matter in vibration. According to the Vedānta, the subtle body, is an undergarment of the soul; the gross physical body is its outer garment. According to the *Taittirīya Upaniṣad*, the soul in man is screened by five sheaths or envelops. The author takes further validation of the existence of soul based on the ideas of "immortality" and "ancestor-worship." The amazing fact of death shows that we exist and die at the same time, because the world we live in is also the world we die.

Majeed Khan and his collaborators have raised a relevant question: Is death an end of life or beginning of a new one? Based on case studies they deal this question in a strictly empirical sense without any admixture of theory. They hold that following the modern science there are two forms of death: "somatic death" and "brain death." The philosophic-religious concept of death is quite different from that of the modern science. The Hindus and the Buddhists adhere to the theory of "reincarnation," while the Muslims and the Christians hold the concept of "eternal afterlife." The authors present two case studies of "experiencing death": Following a major heart attack, a lady was taken to the hospital where she was declared dead. In fact, she was in a coma for three days. On recovery, she narrated that leaving her body she immediately entered a bright tunnel of light where she had a wonderful conversation with God. This gave her a profound understanding not only of man's relationship with God but also how "reincarnation" is true. Another person also described his "near-death experience" of "pure white light," "absence of sound," "extreme peace and serenity," similarity with cosmos and all-life," and specially the feeling of deep regret in having come back to earthly life. Both these personal experiences support the religious belief in a higher state of consciousness where death can be encountered.

K.G. Gurumurthy has examined the religious concept of death among the Liṅgāyats, a religion that came into existence during the twelfth century in south India. The uniqueness of this religion lies in what is known as "Great Opinion," which means not believing in "rebirth," "transmigration of soul" and existence of "many worlds." The Sarana Ligāyat's view of death is different from that of the other religions in so far as they believe that births and deaths are like waves formed and merged on a high sea. This means "man never gets separated from God." On the death of a person the cremation-rite is performed. The Liṅgāyats are the people who receive, wear and worship *Śiva-liṅga,* in an emblem form, moduled in a mixture of black wax and other ingredients. They wear the *iṣṭaliṅga* on their person and thus worship their own body with the sacred ashes and the leaves. The dead body is buried under a pit in a sitting posture holding the *iṣṭaliṅga* in the right palm, as if the person is sitting for Śiva-worship. On this occasion sacred leaves are offered to the dead. No tomb is constructed for a Sarana Liṅgāyat.

Ahmad Sageer Inam Shastri presents the concept of death among the Sūfīs of the Muslim World. Sūfīsm has been a factor for the integration of Hinduism and Islam. The Muslims believe in no-god but God, and Muhammad as their Prophet. There are a number of verses (*surah*) in Holy *Koran* where the subject of death, the day of judgement, hell and heaven find mention. The central belief in Islam is that every soul will have to enter into the realm of death. The soul does not die but the "death of the body" gives a taste of death to the soul. It is God who gives both life and death. He gathers people together for the day of judgement about which there is no doubt. The Sūfīs aspire to gain the "everlasting life after death." They believe that the real life starts only after death.

George Rajmohan cogently argues the Christian belief in resurrection of the body, which establishes not only the immortality of the soul alone but also of the body. There is a point of similarity between Islam and Christianity and difference with the Hindu concept of rebirth and reincarnation. The Christian notion of resurrection glorifies human being as both spiritual and material. Death is not the end of life but the beginning of a new one.

Now such a philosophical interpretation and religious significance of death may draw attention to the belief in "future life." The central belief is that even after the end of one's life there is a continuity in the other world. The anniversary of one's death is, as it were, his birthday in the next. Death is not a destruction of the soul but a mere transference. So what is required in this life for physical maintenance is to have a belief in the next life. On the occasion of the death anniversary food is offered to the deceased, as if alive. Among the Hindus once there was a custom of *satī* performed by the wives in which a widow used to sacrifice herself in the blaze of her husband's pyre. This is an extreme example. Marriage is not a contract among the Hindus; it is a religious sacrament. It is still believed that a pair once united is as if it was for ever. So, in the past, some wives sacrificed their lives to remain united with their husbands. The Parsees, who form a branch of the Indo-Iranian group of people, had a custom that when a husband or wife dies, it is not only of the dying person that the funeral ceremonies are performed but also of surviving partner. The funeral ceremony is known as *sraosh*. In the case, where they are performed in double, i.e., for the husband also, they are spoken of as *joranī kriyā*, i.e., ceremonies of the (married) pairs. Similarly when the husband dies the same ceremonies are repeated for the wife. This view seems to be connected with the belief in "resurrection," which has led Christians, Muslims and others to burial. The ancient Persians had the custom of *astodans* or *ossuries*. The Egyptians followed the custom of mummying, and having subterranean tombs and Pyramids for the mummies. Among the Parsees in India and Persia as also among the Tibetans, there prevailed the custom of exposure of the body to the Sun and to flesh-devouring birds and animals, like vulture. The custom of preserving bones in one form or another has prevailed in most of the countries of Central Asia, China and Japan.

PHYSICAL SCIENCE AND SOCIAL SCIENCE

The assertions of the ancient philosophy and religion, concerning death, may be taken today as superstition, abstract model or at best a working hypothesis. On the other hand, the "science search" and the "social experience" may be regarded today as a "fact." From the viewpoint of biological scientists death is a natural phenomenon governed by the physical laws and independent of all moral, religious and philosophical influences. The actual acceptance of scientific theories has always been a compromise between the technological and the sociological usage of science. Human conduct is influenced by social, religious and political creeds directly, while the influence of science is rather indirect. The common man is not concerned with the validation of scientific theories. Granted that these two levels of enquiry differ, the similarity can also be imagined because experiment and experience form a general viewpoint, eventually capable of pulling down the wall.

P.K. Saraswati examines the theory of "extinction." Two kinds of extinction have been identified. One is "phyletic extinction" or "pseudo extinction" in which case there is no loss of number of species. The other is "true extinction" wherein a species lineage becomes extinct. There are three major concepts related to the death of species. First, transformation from one form to the other. Second, failure to adapt changing environment. Third, killing by natural or extraterrestrial process. The recent developments in the field of molecular biology to clone the extinct animal raise another dimension to the death of species. Do the species ever die?

M.M. Chaturvedi deals with the concept of death in biological systems. He takes up the question of "entropy" which is a thermodynamic term. As the law has it, a disintegrated system with high entropy becomes a part and parcel of a system, that is an isolated one, and is the most stable. But to have a stable system at highest entropy the system should not have any order or shape. Modern science is unable to comprehend it, but traditional thought has an answer. The Indian philosophical concept of *nirākāra Brahman*, the formless order of the Universe, presents a great principle which follows that the system would never die nor would have any shape and yet would have a very high probability of being found everywhere. According to biochemists, life-process is nothing but a sum of complex chemical reactions which eventually come to equilibrium. Hence death is the "equilibrium of life" and life exists to come to its equilibrium. Modern science has addressed itself to understand the mechanism of what is called "cell-death." Every cell is destined to die as it is born loaded with destructive machinery made up of *proteros*, called *caspases*, which is aptly called Yama, the God of Death, perceived in Indian scriptures.

Lavina Chaubey portrays her views on death, derived from life sciences. On a purely scientific ground, death occurs in two stages called "clinical death" and "molecular death." The immediate and the late signs of death have been defined. The purpose of this theory is to serve as an evidence of death. It is important from biological viewpoint to determine the sign of death and the exact time for the disposal of the dead.

Narasimha Murthy presents a comparative study of death in the *Āyurveda* and the life sciences. The author reviews briefly the six basic causes of death and birth as reflected in the *Āyurveda*. The life sciences are not proposing any direct theory in relation to death, but study pathological sequences at seven different levels. From the Indian viewpoint, only a *yogī* can determine the apparent or false death.

L. Tenzin presents the concept and causes of death as reflected in the Tibetan science of medicine. There are two ways of deterring death: "subtle signs of death observed by others," and "subtle signs of death experienced by oneself." A Tibetan physician can predict the imminent death of a patient. There are eight inauspicious and gross signs in the patient, which indicate the impending death. There are also signs of sudden death. Tibetans believe in the law of *karma*, which governs the life-cycle. The five primordial elements constitute the body and also play its role in the destruction of the body. At the very moment of destruction each of these elements is an enemy of every other element and tries to defeat one another letting the body frail. The signs related to motiveless and sudden changes in the behaviour of a person indicate that death may be on the way, despite the fact that one might apparently be in sound health. The signs appearing in dream is also an indicator of the patient's death and future.

Yolotl González Torres, with anthropological background, presents a case study of death in pre-hispanic Mexico. Modern Mexicans are different from the ancient Mexicans. Christianity reduced the ancients to a quite different people. Originally the Mexicans believed that men have been created to serve and nourish the gods. This set forth believing further that souls or "energies" could leave the body during sleep, trance or certain illness or definitely during death. After death the soul of the deceased has to go through a perilous journey. Death rituals vary according to circumstances such as when one dies in battle, dies in water, dies during business and dies of disease. Dead kings were defied. There are several locations associated with the dead. Another set of beliefs presents the future of the dead. Those who desired good food and gaiety go to the land of water and mist, and subsequently return to earth. Some achieve higher perfection, making worthy of living in the house of the Sun. There are other places where the souls of the deceased do not suffer, a common belief among the ancients.

Onkar Prasad presents the anthropological truth of an ancient society. The Santals believe that after death the soul goes to live in a world which is different from that of the earthly one. Death is caused by malignant spirits. Purificatory rites are performed to help the departed soul in distress. The funeral rites are performed to help the departed soul in distress. The rites are aimed at ensuring smooth journey of the soul to the world of ancestors. The fundamental belief in the continuity of life after death strengthens the concept of re-birth, which is essentially an operational character of the Hindu world.

M. Suryanarayana postulates an anthropological theory of death instrumentally verifiable in the case of the Saoras who believe in the immortality of the body with life. This was later pronounced as "immortality of the soul" after the death of the body and the "eternal abode of the fathers." The eternality of life is further supported by a strong belief that snakes, monkeys and baboons "live for ever," unless they are killed. Death is generally attributed to some malignant spirit or wizard. In a given instance the concept of two souls (*puradāna*) further strengthens the theory of immortality. Of the two souls, one is having existence "independent of the body". It is invisible, personal, transmigrant and immortal. It can also leave the body at will and freely wander about, and return to the body of a person to which it belongs.

B.D. Tripathi deals briefly with the sociology (social psychology) of death. Referring to Gautama Buddha's reflection on death, the author points out that the institution of ascetism is the handiwork of death. The Jaina's *prāyopasan* (welcoming death by foregoing food) is a case in point glorifying death. Hindus committing suicide at *kāśikarvaṭ* near Viśvanātha Temple in Varanasi is another example of the reminiscence of that tradition.

Hetukar Jha reflects upon the social reality of "death" and "existence" of man. This conviction of the author apparently comes from the sociological thought that builds up great debates about structure and function which is the key of his interpretation. Both text and context favour the better-adapted sources of the author's thought.

Umesh K. Singh describes death and dying in the socio-cultural milieu of Kāśī, a sacred city, which is believed to ensure liberation (*mokṣa*) from the cycle of birth-and-death. The scriptural sources provide explanations of death, which occupy a central place in Hindu social preception.

In order to obtain a basis from which science and society pronounce judgement about death, one should put a question: "In what sense does science search the truth about death?" The "truth" about death does not consist of "facts," because it is not empirically verifiable, as students of anthropology and sociology would like to trace back. In traditional thought the laws of science are also the laws of ethics. There is a connection between the desirable human conduct and the divine laws of the universe. The interpretation of death, in support of moral rules and higher generality, is well known to traditional societies. Those who deny any connection between scientific theories and religious beliefs fail to appreciate the logic of the human mind. The Indian concept of *mokṣa* is close to the modern science theory of "extinction" (*mokṣa*). The concept of *nirākāra Brahman* helps understand the thermodynamic term "entropy." The voices that have raised questions on the subject of death will continue so long as mankind survives. It would be a mistake to believe that the modern science has rejected the traditional theory of death. This exercise has demonstrated as to how this hard-headed research can illuminate a certain theory that serves as a bridge between the physical science and the social science. The purpose of this exercise has been to speak about the most overall general character of Nature and the nature of Man. Such a topic as death has a tendency to become too philosophical and sentimental because one cannot say what happens after death. The stage after death is not apparent to the eye but only to the eye of an analyst.

Part I
Philosophy and Religion

1

Upaniṣadic Concept of Death

R.C. Sharma

SINCE the dawn of civilization man has engaged himself in unfolding the layers of the deep mystery of death. The scintillating and varied efforts made throughout the globe open a vast horizon for interesting and multiple researches, yet the riddle continues to be unsolved to date. The Indian sages, seers and path-finders have dwelt upon this enigma quite absorbedly and shed sparkling light through their insight and vision.

The Upaniṣadic thinkers who were aspirants to be conversant with the puzzles of life and the Supreme Being, *brahma-jijñāsā*, were also curious to know beyond, i.e., the stage after its termination or extinction of what we call "death" (*mṛtyu*). For them it was not a horrifying event but an essential occurrence, which was to come sooner or later, and one was to be prepared to face, to receive or welcome it. The Upaniṣads of course aim at *amṛta* but this is not the nectar or juice, which does not allow death to come but this *amṛta* is the bliss which makes the life divine and after reaching this stage death does not mean anything. It is the end of one journey and beginning of the other.

When the *Īśāvāsya* or *Īśa Upaniṣad* (11) says:

अविद्या मृत्युंतीर्त्वा विद्याऽमृतमश्नुते ॥

The message seems to disseminate that a man has to cross the ocean of ignorance (which is like death) through his efforts and aspire for attainment of Supreme Knowledge which is like tasting of *amṛta* and this is the goal of every person. The word *avidyā* has been explained differently but it seems to denote human efforts (seeing of action). It can thus be explained that one has to make efforts to overcome death and the next stage will be "knowledge."

The life emerges from *agni* or light and enters into the same element after death.

तं प्रेतं दिष्टमितोऽग्नय एव हरन्ति यत एवेतो संभूतो भवति

— *Chāndogya*, 5.9.2

It is for this reason that at the time of passing away of a person, God Pūṣan is invoked. This deity is the glowing substance of the Sun. Thus the beaming light of fire or sun becomes the mediator to carry the soul from one body to the other or from this world to the next. As such where is the occasion of mourning or lamentation? After all ". . . death is the cessation of the Manifest . . . through negation of the manifest man overcomes death."[1] This itself is a great experience. The concluding three hymns of *Īśāvāsya* (15, 17-18).[2]

The dying person is not perturbed. He reconciles with this moment rather happily but prays for bestowing real knowledge for his journey beyond.

हिरण्मयेन पात्रेण सत्यस्यापिहितं मुखम्।
तत्त्वं पूषन्नपावृणु सत्य धर्माय दृष्टये॥

— *Īśa*, 15

With golden vessel the face of the Real is covered over; that do thou, O Pūṣan, uncover, that I, devoted to the truth may behold.[3]

---

1. Rohit Mehta, *The Call of the Upaniṣads*, Reprint, 1990, p. 27.
2. Bettina Bäumer, "The Concluding Mantras of Īśāvāsya Upaniṣad with Special Reference to Pūṣan" (*Īśa*, 15-17), *Jñāna-Pravāha Bulletin* no. 5, 2001-2.
3. Rohit Mehta, *op cit.*, p. 29.

The person at the time of death realizes that during lifetime the "Truth" could not be realized in its proper perspective, as it remained concealed within a veil of gold or worldly allurements. He therefore, requests, Pūṣan to remove the golden veil and help in knowing the "Truth" at least in the next birth or in the next stage following the cessation of body. The next hymn (no. 16) is also a prayer to Pūṣan. He then requests for disintegration of different components of body into their elements.

> वायुरनिलममृतमथेदं भस्मान्तँ शरीरम्।
> ॐ क्रतो स्मर कृतँ स्मर क्रतो स्मर कृतँ स्मर॥
>
> — *Īśa*, 17

> The vital breath may enter into ever pervading water and the body may (enter into the fire to) become ash and you may please remember my deeds.

The last hymn is prayer to the fire god, Agni, to lead through the good path (to reach the goal of Truth).

> अग्ने नय सुपथा राये अस्मान् विश्वानि देव वयुनानि विद्वान्
>
> — *Īśu*, 18

Offering of the body to the fire is the last function of life and this also clears the path for the beginning of another and better journey of life.

The *Kaṭhopaniṣad* presents an interesting episode relating to death and its presiding deity, Yama. Naciketā himself knocks at the door of Yama and questions him, among other things, about the stage after death as people are generally confused:

> येयं प्रेते विचिकित्सा मनुष्येऽस्तीत्येके नायमस्तीति चैके।
> एतद्विद्यामनुशिष्टस्त्वयाऽहं वराणामेष वरस्तृतीयः॥
>
> — *Kaṭha*, 1.20

Yama discourages Naciketā as it is an extremely secret issue and even gods remain curious in this regard. The query should, therefore, be withdrawn and substituted by another one. Naciketā even being repeatedly discouraged and allured for some other boon insists to be conversant with this knotty riddle.

Yama ultimately agrees to explain and says that there are two paths, one depending on the good deeds, *śreyas*, and the other longing for pleasures, *preyas*. The former attains immortal goal while the latter perishes. "One who realizes the Supreme Truth, he becomes free from the fetters of the world. He is neither born, nor dies."[4] The god of death behaves well with boy Naciketā and preaches him like an enlightened teacher. He further elaborates his viewpoint that at the time of leaving a body and simultaneously obtaining the other person, the soul enters the *yoni* as per his deeds:

योनिमन्ये प्रपद्यन्ते शरीरत्वाय देहिनः।
स्थाणुमन्येऽनुसंयन्ति यथा कर्म तथा श्रुतम्॥
— *Kaṭha*, 2.2.7

Sage Pippalāda responding to the query of Sukeśā in the *Praśnopaniṣad* (6.6) states that one who realizes the Puruṣa is not afraid of death. We are informed through the *Aitareya Upaniṣad* that God created several planets including that of death — *maram* or *maraḥ* (*AitUp*, 1.1.2). The god of death is supposed to dwell in the navel:

. . . मृत्युरपानो भूत्वा नाभिं प्राविशत् . . .
— *Ibid*, 1.2.4

When the seer of *Taittirīya Upaniṣad* conceives of a Supreme Deity directing other gods in their functions death is also one of the five ("मृत्युर्धावति पंचम इति" — *Taitt.*, 2.8)

It has further been suggested that at the time of death one leaves this body and attains different microforms from *anna* to *ātmā*. This Upaniṣad reveals that if a deity is worshipped as

---

4. J.K. Sadani, *Wisdom of Upaniṣads*, 1993, p. 15.

appointed by God to annihilate the same may be invoked to kill foes.[5]

In the *Śvetāśvatara Upaniṣad* we come across the concept of Kālākāla, i.e., death[6] and this later culminated into Mahākāla of Śaivism and is also manifested in the Brāhmaṇical and Buddhist iconography, looking fierce and fearful.

We find numerous references relating to death in the *Chāndogya Upaniṣad.* Āruṇi Uddālaka explains to his son Śvetaketu that at the time of death the speech is merged in the mind, mind in *prāṇa* (vital breath), *prāṇa* in light and light in the Ultimate Reality (*ātman* or *paramātman*):

पुरुषस्य प्रयतो वाङ्मनसि सम्पद्यते, मनः प्राणे,
प्राणस्तेजसि, तेजः परस्यां देवतायाम।

— *Chāndogya,* VI.8.6, 15.1-2

This phenomenon has further been made explicit through the simile of collection of honey by the bees. After the juice is collected the identity of the trees is merged or lost. Similarly when a person after death is merged with the Supreme Soul his own identity is lost:

यथा सोम्य मधु मधुकृतो निस्तिष्ठन्ति नानात्ययानां वृक्षाणां
रसान्समवहारमेकता रसं गमयन्ति।
. . . इमाः सर्वा प्रजाः सति सम्पद्य न विदुः सति सम्पद्यामह इति।

— *Ibid.,* VI.9.1-2

Prajāpati explains to Indra that the body is mortal but it is also the carrier of immortal and bodiless soul, which experiences sorrows and happiness till it remains with body. When it becomes bodiless sufferings and pleasures do not touch it:

मर्त्यं वा इदं शरीरमात्तं मृत्युना तदस्यामृतस्य अशरीरस्यात्मनोऽधिष्ठानम्
आत्तो वै शरीरः प्रियाप्रियाभ्याम् . . . —*Ibid.,* VIII.12.1

5. *Taittirīya Upaniṣad,* 3.10.

6. *Śvetāśvataropaniṣad,* 6.2.

> The *Bṛhadāraṇyaka Upaniṣad* puts forth an interesting observation that the son represents his father upon his death and some ritual just before expiry is prescribed.[7] "When a man thinks he will die, he says to his son — you are *Brahman*, you are the sacrifice and you are the world. — The son replies, "I am *Brahman*, I am sacrifice and I am the world . . ." "When a father who knows as above departs from this world, he penetrates his son together with the organ of speech, the mind and the vital force. Should anything be left undone by him through any slip the son exonerates him from all that. Therefore, he is called son. Divine and immortal speech, mind and vital force permeate him."[8]

Similar episode is cited in the *Kauṣītaki Upaniṣad* (2.14) where a dying man waits for death rather rejoicing and summons his son to transmit his merits to his son. It is just like the handing down the heritage from one generation to the other. He whispers in his son's ear in the end "I would lay in you all my life forces" and the son responds "I receive in me your life forces."

In the assembly of erudite brāhmaṇas convened by Janaka, Aśvala enquired from Yājñavalkya that life has to be taken away by death and everything is within the reach of extinction then how a *yajña* can liberate a person from death? To this replies Yājñavalkya that it is through fire that one overcomes the death. Speech by its very nature is fire and sacrificer's organ of speech is *hotṛ*. The trinity of fire, speech and sacrificer helps one to be liberated and he enjoyed the stage, which is beyond the clutches of death.[9]

---

7. *Bṛhadāraṇyaka Upaniṣad*, IV.17
8. *Ibid*, tr. by Svāmī Mādhavānanda, 1988, p. 160.
9. " . . . यदिदं सर्व मृत्युनाप्तं, सर्वं मृत्युनाभिपन्नं केन यजमानो मृत्योराप्तिमतिमुच्यत इति। होत्रर्त्विजाग्निना वाचा, वाग्वै यज्ञस्य होता, तद्येयं वाक् सोऽयमग्निः, स होता, स मुक्तिः, सातिमुक्तिः" — *Ibid*. III.1.3

These are only a few citations from the important and early Upaniṣads. On their perusal we may conclude as under:

(1) Death is not a fearful or horrifying event. It is an essential phase of life and has to be accepted like other occasions.

(2) The seers of Upaniṣads are often seen well-prepared to receive, better to say, welcome death. The reason seems that they have already detached themselves from the bodily bondage and for them, life and death are two sides of the same medallion. This thought has handed down from the early Vedic tradition.[10]

(3) The reason of this joyous feeling even at the time of death seems that the dying person is satisfied with his contribution and attainments of his life-span. No more desires are left to be fulfilled. This aspect is seen reflected in the Gupta period gold coins and the legend that narrates that the king has won the world and through his noble deeds he also wins the paradise:

क्षितिपतिः गामवजित्य सुचरितैर्दिवं जयति।

(4) The seer of Upaniṣad is quite friendly with the god of death and no iota of fear penetrates his mind. This is particularly noticed in the conversation between Naciketā and Yama.

(5) Thinkers of the Upaniṣadic period long for immortality not by reserving their seat in Heavens but through becoming one with the Supreme and therefore, they were always keen to unfold the mysteries of life, death, *ātman* and *Brahman*: अथातो ब्रह्म जिज्ञासा. This stage represents the strength of character which made them fearless.

(6) Death is not the extinction of life but it opens a horizon for a new journey or birth on this planet or the other.

---

10. यस्यं छायामृतं यस्य मृत्युः कस्मैं देवाय हविषा विधेम॥ — *ṚV*, X.121.2

(7) Both life and death begin and end with fire or light and therefore death follows birth and birth follows death. Both should be greeted. This concept is reflected in the early Buddhist and Jain *stūpa*s, which illuminated with thousands of lamps. The demise of the Buddha or Jaina symbolized the freedom from the cycle of birth and death, the coveted goal of the pontiff, hence the event was to be rejoiced.

(8) The horrifying picture of *naraka* and god of death appears to be a late concept; or we can safely say even if it had some origin in the early phase,[11] it developed through ages. Of course, we are confronted with the term *kālākāla* (Reference no. 6).

(9) With the passage of time vices crept into people and it was deemed necessary to warn them to be away from evils which could inject harm to the society also. Hence, the philosophy of horrifying *naraka* and fearful deity Yama are sometimes explained or illustrated as Māhākāla.

---

11. यौ ते श्वानौ यमरक्षितारौ चतुरक्षौ पथिरक्षी नृचक्षसौ।
ताभ्यामेनं परि देहि राजन् त्स्वस्ति चात्मा अनमीवं च धेहि॥

उरूणसावसुतृपा उदुम्बलौ यमस्य दूतौ चरतो जनां अनु।
तावस्मभ्यं दृशये सूर्याय पुनर्दातामसुमद्येह भद्रम्॥ — *Ṛ͏V*, X.14.10-11

2

Meditation on Death

Bettina Bäumer

The face of Truth is covered over
By a golden vessel. Uncover it, O Lord,
That I who love the truth may see.

O Lord, sole Seer, Controller, Sun,
Son of the Father of beings, shine forth.
Concentrate your splendour that I may behold
Your most glorious form. He who is yonder —
The Man yonder — I myself am He!

Go, my breath, to the immortal wind,
Then may this body end in ashes!
Remember, O my mind, the deeds of past,
Remember the deeds, remember the deeds!

— *Īśa*, 15-17

(tr. R. Panikkar, *The Vedic Experience*)

DEATH is a universal theme in all traditions of mankind but modern Western civilization has suppressed it and hidden it under a cover of medical technology. However, a renewed interest can be found in a conscious reflection on death, taking the help of spiritual traditions such as Tibetan Buddhism. In India, one of the earliest texts preparing man to die and leading him to the state transcending death is the *Īśa Upaniṣad*, which is even today recited at the occasion of death.

The last four verses of the *Īśa Upaniṣad* have been variously called a prayer of a dying person. The last verse (18) being a *mantra* from the *Ṛgveda* (1.189.1), I shall limit my meditation to the three verses (15-17) which contain in a nutshell the ultimate prayers of the dying as well as of the living. The link with death is established through verse 14 immediately preceding:

> *vināśena mṛtyuṁ tīrtvā saṁbhutyāmṛtam aśnute.*
>
> The man who understands both the impermanent and the permanent holding the two in tension together, the impermanent passes over death and by the permanent attains immortal life.

Generally only verses 15 and 16 are attributed to the dying person, and 17 appears to be the reflection and invocation of the living, the survivors or relatives.

What is striking is the strong invocation of Pūṣan in these two *mantra*s. Strangely, Pūṣan, a Vedic deity, disappears in the Upaniṣads after these powerful verses which occur in the parallel passages of *Bṛhadāraṇyaka* (5.15) and *Īśa*.

Verse 15 starts with the statement that the face of truth is covered with a golden vessel: *hiraṇmayena pātreṇa satyasya apihitaṁ mukham*. The "golden vessel" has invariably been interpreted as the sun which covers the Ultimate, the Real: *satyam*. In the same verse there are two levels of *satya*: the ultimate truth or Reality which lies beyond and with which the dying person has to identify him/herself. This is only possible if the person is already dedicated to the ultimate truth and reality, if he/she is *satya dharma*. The final obstacle to see the Real is the sun itself and the divinity invoked to remove this obstacle is Pūṣan. He is addressed very personally: *tvam pūṣan apāvṛṇu*, showing a kind of familiarity, even intimacy with this divinity. Not by chance the following *mantra* starts with an invocation of Pūṣan.

Before continuing an exegeses of the *mantra*s, we should throw some light on the Vedic deity and discover why he is foremost in being invoked in the process of dying. We shall see that the many faceted and yet unitary figure of Pūṣan holds the key to the understanding of *mantra*s 15-16 of the *Īśa.*

One important aspect of Pūṣan's nature which opens up the meaning of these *mantra*s is his relation to the Sūrya and hence to light and illumination. The three aspects of the Sun are: "Sūrya, the sun in manifestation, Pūṣan, the glowing innermost essence of this manifestation, and Savitṛ, the impeller." (Stella Kramrisch, p. 160) Pūṣan is always called the radiant or glowing one (*āghṛṇi*) in the Veda and he is the personification of the glowing substance of the sun, impelled by Savitṛ. That there is a difference between the manifest sun, Sūrya and its innermost glowing nature, becomes clear in verse 15 because the manifestation, even of light, becomes an obstacle hiding the ultimate essence, the inner light and truth. Pūṣan, having gone beyond to the higher realms of light, is the true and fitting mediator at the moment of death or illumination.

The connection with light is also related to vision (*dhī*) and Pūṣan is the all-seeing deity (cf. *ṚV*, III.62.9). It is, therefore, only fitting that he is invoked for a clear vision. This implies also a removal of obstacle (*tvam pūṣan apāvṛṇu . . . dṛṣṭaye*), his another important function. He removes obstacles of all kinds, and foremost he is a guide and fore-runner on all paths, a path-finder:

> Shorten our path, O Pūṣan, remove all stumbling blocks, Deliverer.
> Be at hand to guide.
>
> — *ṚV*, 1.4.1

He shows the way and smoothens the paths not only in this world but also in the way to the beyond, guiding the souls of the departed to the world of the Fathers.

Death has been considered as a journey in practically all religious traditions. Pūṣan is the guide on the path and he was even born on the pathway:

> On distant pathways is the birth place of Pūṣan,
> remote from heaven, remote from earth.

> To the two abodes that are dear to his heart,
> He comes, then departs, knowing each path.
> He knows and traverses each heavenly realm.
> May he guide us in ways that are wholly secure!
> Undertaking our welfare, shielding from all harm —
> May he who knows lead the way with vigilance!
>
> — *Atharvaveda*, VII.91-2
> (tr. R. Panikkar)

The symbolism used in the *Īśa* does not speak directly of a journey but it is implied and the very invocation of Pūṣan is a reminder of his role of perfect guide and charioteer (*Ṛgveda*, VI.55.2; VI.56.2-3), as the protector and guardian on the final journey. He is therefore not only a remover of the dangers and obstacles but a liberator (*vimocana*) (*Ṛgveda*, I.42.1; VIII. 4.15-16). He delivers also from sin (*Atharvaveda*, VI.112.3), an important aspect at the moment of death.

Stella Kramrisch summarizes some of the important functions of Pūṣan thus:

> All the while Pūṣan glows in the ardour of his nature, a steady guide who, on his way, never loses any of his heard, finds hidden treasures and nourishes and ripens all. — p. 161

And again:

> The glowing one moves undiminished on his paths. He illumines and liberates. He guides, finds and gives. — p. 175

His role in leading the souls to their final abode is further described in the *Ṛgveda* (VI.54.7): "May none be injured, may none be destroyed in the pit, rather arrive with them unharmed." Pūṣan is also the Lord of the threshold. In the Gṛhyasūtras, Pūṣan is associated with crossing the threshold of a house (*ŚGS*, 2.14.9; *Vedic Mythology*, p. 36). He is invoked on one's beginning of a journey and when one calls on him when one loses the way (*AGS*, 3.7.8-9; *ibid.*).

Death is a journey and a threshold and both need special protection as moments of transition and passages from one condition to another.

The only epithet used for Pūṣan in the *Īśa* is *ekarṣi*, "the one (sole) seer," which has been applied to the sun but it has also a mystical meaning. He is the one seer who has the unitary and single vision. In both verses, 15 and 16, Pūṣan is invoked for a clear and total vision (*dhī*, cf. Gonda, *The Vision of the Vedic Poets*, p. 86f.). "The guardian of the pathways (Pūṣan) is (in *ṚV*, VI.49.8) implored for being every *dhīḥ* to fulfilment" (p. 87).

After calling upon Pūṣan as the *ekarṣi*, a term that occurs only rarely in the Upaniṣads (cf. *Muṇḍaka*, III.2.10, Olivelle, p. 453), verse 16 then invokes Yama and Sūrya. Prājāpatya, son of Prajāpati, can refer to either of these deities since they are created by Prajāpati. The invocation of these deities together seems like a more powerful outburst of the person on the point of death. After the collection of vocatives, the *mantra* contains an intense prayer and an exclamation.

The prayer consists of the four words: "Spread out your rays and collect your glory" (*vyūha raśmīn samūha tejaḥ*). It is as if the dying person is blinded by the light and as in the previous verse, the light of the sun and the transcendent light are two levels of the same light-filled reality. Death is an encounter with light, as almost all spiritual traditions confirm, but a light that can be unbearable. The first part of the prayer may be a continuation of the prayer to Pūṣan in verse 15, namely to uncover the face of the Real which is hidden by the sun through *Vyūha raśmīn* "spreading out" or opening up the rays, so that the dying person can see what lies beyond. The vision of the dying has to be unified in the ultimate light which is not the multiplicity of the rays which illumine the external world. This process of unification is expressed by the second half: *samūha tejaḥ*, "collect, gather, draw in your brilliance." Pūṣan is the deity who gathers the light in the glowing, radiant energy which is the essence of the sun, as we have seen. The dying person has to identify him/herself with this glory, radiance and energy (*tejas*) which lies beyond all the visible forms of light (*jyotiṣāṃ jyoti* in the

Bhagavad-Gītā, 13.17). The two movements expressed in this prayer could be said to relate to the overcoming of multiplicity and the unification of the effulgent glory which is the essence of light.

Hume says in a note on his passage: "At best the passage is of obscure mystical significance." (p. 364) Though he is right that the phrase has a mystical significance, I would like to add that the mystical experience is not necessarily obscure or only for those who have not had it. On the contrary, it is the clearest way of preceiving reality. The last *mantras* of the *Īśa* dealing with the ultimate experience, whether death or mystical insight, indicate it in a brief and condensed language which makes it difficult to interpret.

The second half of verse 16 is no longer a prayer but a mystical exclamation: from imperative it moves to direct present tense: *paśyāmi, asmi.* It is again addressed to a "thou" (*tvam* of verse 15): *te.* Who is addressed here, since the verse starts with the invocation of three divinities: Pūṣan, Yama and Sūrya? It appears that it is actually Pūṣan who is meant and Yama and Sūrya are his aspects in this context (there are sufficient references in the *Ṛgveda* on the close relation between Pūṣan, Yama and Sūrya). The mystical exclamation consists of two phases: *yatte rūpaṃ kalyāṇatamaṃ tatte paśyāmi* is the first. It is a vision of the supremely beautiful and auspicious divine form. *Kalyāṇa* is much more than beautiful, it is that which bestows goodness and salvation. This vision is the result of the concentrated glory (*samūha tejas*) and yet there is a jump, a gap between the two halves of the verse. It is in this gap that the mystical experience happens. A similar gap can be found in the famous *mantra* of the *Taittirīya*:

> Whence words recoil, together with the mind,
> without having attained it —
> whoever knows this bliss of *Brahman* has no fear.
>
> — *Taittirīya*, 2.4.1

The actual experience happens in this gap where words fail and language becomes powerless. Only afterwards an exclamaion follows as the effect. The vision expressed by *paśyāmi* (I see) is of a divine "thou" who is not an individual deity but a concentration of that divine light.

The first part is a divine vision which still has an object, a form, but the second part is an identification:

> *yo'sāvasau puruṣaḥ so'ham asmi*
>
> He who is that divine Person beyond, I am He!

We are reminded of a parallel *mantra* of the *Śvetāśvatara*:

> I have known that mighty Person, golden like the sun, beyond all darkness. By knowing him a man transcends death; there is no other path for reaching the goal.

In both the cases it is a moment of vision-and-identification with the glorious, resplendent Divine Person, beyond darkness and death. Both *mantra*s describe the very experience by which death is transcended. "Knowing" in the Upaniṣads is always a becoming: *ya evaṃ veda sa eva bhavati* is the frequent phrase. The transcendence of the *puruṣa* is expressed in *Īśa* (16) by repeating: *asau asau,* "beyond, beyond."

So'ham asmi: "I am he" is the culmination of this process of vision-and-identification, a culmination which may occur at the moment of death or enlightenment. *So'ham* has become the famous *haṁsa-mantra* in many spiritual schools, but here it is at its origin. The identification with the true and utimate "I," *aham*, is the condition for transcending death. At the origin it is the self-awareness of the *ātman*, as in the *Bṛhadāraṇyaka Upaniṣad* (I.4.1):

> In the beginning this world was just a single self (*ātman*) shaped like a man. He looked around and saw nothing but himself. The first thing he said was, "Here I am!" and from that the name "I" came into being. Therefore, even today when you call someone, he first says, "It's I," and then states whatever other name he may have. That first being received the name "man" (*puruṣa*), because ahead (*pūrva*) of all this he burnt up (*uṣ*) all evils.
>
> — tr. P. Olivelle

But in the *Īśa* and its parallel in the *Bṛhadāraṇyaka* it is the final identification with the *aham*, with the divine *puruṣa;* in terms of Kashmir Śaivism we could say it is the act of recognition (*pratyabhijñā*) of one's real (*aham-svarūpa*): *so'ham asmi*.

The first expression of vision is addressed to a "thou": *te rūpam*, and the second is in the third person: *saḥ*. As there seems to be a mix-up between Pūṣan, Yama, Sūrya and Puruṣa, there seems to be a mix-up of the personal pronouns: first, second and third person. This apparent mix-up can only be understood in mystical experience.

The Upaniṣadic *mantra* being extremely brief, we may take the help of Abhinavagupta for its exegesis. I am referring to a passage in his *Parātriṁśikā Vivaraṇa* where he analyses the interrelatedness of the three grammatical persons. We cannot go here into the details of his grammatical, philosophical and mystical argumentation but the conclusion is this: the three persons are not separate, but interrelated, and there is an order of ascension from the third (*idam, saḥ*), to the second (*tvam*) and ultimately they merge in the first person (*aham*). (*PTV*, Jaideva Singh, pp. 70 ff. Engl. tr., p. 25 ff. of Sanskrit text)

In the light of Abhinavagupta's analysis of language, the *mantra* of the *Īśa* is a perfect example of the interrelatedness of the three persons and of the final merging of the second and third persons in the first: *so'ham asmi*.

Since the *mantra* is traditionally associated with the moment of dying, we find a similar situation in the eschatological description of the *Kauṣītaki Upaniṣad* (1.5):

> There the journey of the soul to the Brahma-world is described in more mythological terms. After passing through several stages and stations, the soul reaches the throne of *Brahman* who asks: "Who are you?" The soul first gives its identity with the body but then goes on to give its real identity: "What you are, this I am" (*yastvam asi so'ham asmi*, I.6). He is further questioned by *Brahman*: "Who am I?" to which he answers: "the Real (truth, *satyam*)." This can be linked with *Īśa* (15) where it is *satyam* which has to be uncovered, revealed for the final vision to become possible.

This last part of verse 16 is the culmination of the prayer of the dying person, the attainment or recognition of his identity with the divine *puruṣa,* the light beyond the sun and beyond darkness. What remains is the last *mantra* (verse 17), leaving aside the quotation from *Ṛgveda* (18):

> *vāyuranilam amṛtamathedaṁ bhasmāntaṁ śarīram*
>
> Let the breath enter the immortal wind,
> Let the body end in ashes.

The breath of the dying person goes to wind which is the immortal element in man. While his *prāṇa-vāyu* remains immortal, the body ends in ashes. We need not go into the various conceptions in the Upaniṣads relating to the immortal and mortal elements of man but at this stage the immortal element is breath. The phrase is like a general statement about death, it is neither put in the mouth of the dying person nor of the living who accompanies the dying. The last line of verse 17 is addressed by the survivors, relatives and friends to the dying or dead person:

> *oṁ krato smara kṛtaṁ smara krato smara kṛtaṁ smara*
>
> Remember, my mind, the deeds, remember. . .

The repetition indicates the end — the end of life and also the end of the Upaniṣad. The key to the understanding of this phrase is the term *kratu,* which has been translated as "purpose" (Hume) or "mind" (Olivelle) but which has a multiplicity of meanings: intention, resolution, purpose, desire, will, intelligence, understanding, inspiration, enlightenment and also sacrificial rite.

What is the human faculty that has the capacity to remember the past deeds at the moment of death? What remains at that moment is only an intuitive insight, pure intentionality and desire for liberation from all bondage. But the key to the meaning of *kratu* is found in the *Chāndogya Upaniṣad* in the teaching of Śāṇḍilya on death (3.14) which speaks of man as *kratumaya*:

> Now, then, man is undoubtedly made of resolve. What a man becomes on departing from here after death is in accordance with his resolve in this world. So he should make this resolve:
>
> . . . "This self (*ātman*) of mine that lies deep within my heart, it contains all actions, all desires, all smells and all tastes; it has captured this whole world; it neither speaks nor pays any heed. It is *Brahman*. On departing from here after death, I will become that." A man who has this resolve is never beset at all with doubts.
>
> — tr. P. Olivelle

The *kratu* which is described in this passage is much more than a resolve, an intention or desire, it is an all-embracing meditation on life-and-death, a kind of insight compressed in a total understanding of life. This *kratu* is the condition for becoming one with that total Reality of *Brahman* at the time of death (3.14.4).

Thus, the admonition to the dying or dead to remember his deeds also refers to an instantaneous insight into the whole life at the moment of death, a recollection, and by that very act of recollection the effect of the past deeds is overcome. *Smṛti* is also more than memory, it is a kind of meditative recollection, an act of awareness. The whole act which is conjured up in this urge to remember one's past deeds is not an act of the mind or reflective memory, it lies much deeper, at the very threshold between life and death.

I may now attempt an interpretation of the three *mantras* together in relation to death. The Ultimate Reality or truth is hidden from our view and that very veil may be our past actions which prevent us from seeing. To remove this obstacle we need the assistance and grace of the Divine, who is a personification of the light transcending all other lights, such as the light of the sun. Pūṣan is here the guide on this path and liberator and he is rightly invoked in the two *mantras* attributed to the dying as the mediator *par excellence*.

At the moment of death, a realization of one's true being has to take place, and this is the discovery of one's identity with the Divine Person (*puruṣa*), whose vision is most glorious, beautiful and saving (*kalyāṇatamam*). It is a vision leading to identification.

Once this ultimate experience takes place, what remains of a person is the body which returns to the earth element in the form of ashes, and his breath, which merges in the universal and immortal wind. What remains is also his *karma* which can be burnt up in the very act of recollecting it, since the true identity is already discovered:

yo'sāvasau puruṣaḥ so'ham asmi!

References

Abhinavagupta, *Parātriṁśikā-Vivaraṇa*, ed. and tr. Jaideva Singh, Delhi MLBD 1988.

Eighteen Principal Upaniṣads, ed. V.P. Limaye and R.D. Vadekar, Poona, Vaidika Samsodhana Mandala, 1958.

Gonda, J., *The Vision of the Vedic Poets*, Delhi, Munshiram Manoharlal, 1984.

Hume, R.E., *The Thirteen Principal Upaniṣads*, Delhi, OUP, 1983.

Kramrisch, Stella, "Pūṣan" in B. Stoler Miller (ed.), *Exploring India's Sacred Art*, Philadelphia, University of Pennsylvania Press, 1983, pp. 159-77.

Macdonell, A., *The Bṛhad-Devatā*, Delhi, Motilal Banarsidass, 1994 (reprint).

Macdonell, A.A., *Vedic Mythology*, Delhi, MLBD, 1995.

Oberlies, Th., *Die Religion des Ṛgveda*, Vienna, 1998.

Olivelle, P., *The Early Upaniṣad*s, Delhi, MLBD, 1998.

Panikkar, R., *The Vedic Experience*, Delhi, MLBD, 1983.

3

Mystery of Death

K.N. Sahay

General

THE *Kaṭha Upaniṣad*, while talking about the "secret of Death," tells that there is a doubt that when a man dies — some say that he is gone for ever and does not exist, while others hold that he still lives. Which of the two is true? (Abhedananda, 1960: 6). "We do not have the eyes with which we could see beyond the frontiers of wordly life and find out what lies on beyond. . . ." (Maududi, 1979: 3). It is indeed a pertinent question which is baffling

In the *Mahābhārata* Yudhiṣṭhira tells: "In spite of the fact that everyday and day-after-day, animals and human beings are passing out of life, yet we never think of death. We think that we shall never die" (Abhedananda, 1960: 24). "It is a most wonderful thing in the world" (Vivekananda, 1955: 1). "Of the many riddles that have perplexed the intellect of man, in all climes and times, the most intricate is he himself" (*Ibid.*: 8).

There are various sections of the society — saints, sinners, prophets, priests, kings, beggars or commoners — everywhere from the beginning and in all climes, have remained the curiosities to know "what remains after death" (Abhedananda, 1960: 8).

> Modern physiologists, anatomists, pathologists and a host of other materialists and agnostic thinkers . . . hold that body or the

> combination of matter produces thought, intelligence, consciousness, mind or soul. They teach that thought, or intelligence, or consciousness, is nothing but a function of the brain. . . .
>
> — *Ibid.*: 9-10

> Death is an involuntary or *voluntary* switching off of the life current from the bulb of flesh. Yogis who know how to operate the switch of the heart and to control their heart beats, can quit the body quickly or stay as long as they wish.
>
> — Yogananda, 1970: 12

The study of life beyond death as such cannot cover within the realm of "scientific truth." There are some aspects which were experimented and thus became scientific, but there are others which are still paradoxes. We have to think different types of truth or realities which although they may not be scientific but still are highly relevant in the society.

The Sāṁkhya system of Indian Philosophy talks about three types of proof (*pramāṇa*), viz., *pratyakṣa*, *anumāna* and *śabda pramāṇa* (Sahay, 1998: 14). "Scientific truth" comes through experimentation under laboratory conditions; "Conventional truth" is based on direct experiences through sense-organs; and *śabda pramāṇa* is based on scriptures. The last one is a "spiritual science" working with spiritual laws. Apart from it, there are realities which have bearing with "folk traditions" which cannot be ignored.

Philosophy and Religious Texts

There are atheistic and agnostic thinkers like Cārvāka who do not believe in the existence of the soul after death of the body. There are 'Cārvākas' in almost every country, and such followers are spreading very rapidly. They do not "believe in the existence of the soul as separate from the body, or appearing in a life after death." They condemn others as "ignorant and superstitious fools. . ." (Abhedananda, 1960: 6-7).

According to Vedānta philosophy, "the source of conscious-ness cannot be found in matter but may stand independent of it. What we call matter is only the medium through which consciousness manifest itself" (*Ibid*.: 13-14). Further, Vedānta tells that "matter or object is only one half of the universe and the other half is mind or subject or soul." (*Ibid*.: 12)

The Buddhists say that "the body is the cause of mind and intelligence, that consciousness is the result of the combination of insentient matter and unintelligent forces of physical nature." (*Ibid*.: 12) Human life does not end with the death. It relates to either rebirth or *nirvāṇa* (Tiwari, 1983: 57).

Orthodox Christianity looks at death "as the terrible enemy of life," and is "stereotyped." A person is doomed either to enjoy all the pleasures or to go to eternal perdition and suffer for ever (Abhedananda, 1960: 187). Roman Catholic Christians believe that after man is dead, he goes to "purgatory" (*śodhaka agni*) which is like "temporary hell." It is very difficult to say who will go to the purgatory and who will not. A purgatory is an intermediate stage where the soul has to wait till the time of great destruction when there would be nothing except fire. Christ would visit the dead for his last judgement of humanity. The dead bodies would come alive during that judgement and then the souls will be finally sent to the ever-lasting hell, fire or eternal life and the kingdom of God according to their respective good and bad deeds. That is why Catholics invariably pray for all the dead souls of their relatives. By offering rosary and other prayers, they believe to bring *daṇḍamocana* and minimize the period of their stay in purgatory. One may also earn *daṇḍamocana* for himself (Sahay, 1976: 356).

Bible (II Corn., 4: 16) tells that "though our outward man perishes, the inward man is renewed day by day." Thus the ultimate optimism of the *Bible* rests squarely upon a provisional pessimism. The ultimate optimism of the *Bible* always grows out of the recognition and acceptance of the worst that can happen (Mandrelle, 1995: 22). In ancient Hebrew people never disturbed their equanimity by questioning themselves about the soul. "With them death ended all." (Vivekananda, 1955: 11).

> The Egyptians believed in a 'double' which was like a shadow of the body and which remained as long as the body remained. This gave rise to the idea of mummifying the bodies of the dead. If the body was injured in any part, the double or the soul, was likewise injured: so to keep the soul intact they preserved the bodies. — Abhedananda, 1960: 21.

The Mohammedans, Zoroastrians as well as Christians believe in a heaven of all kinds of sense-enjoyments, where pleasures will come incessantly without troubles or any sort of pain. This, according to the Hindus, is not a desirable state" (*Ibid.*: 20).

Writers of the most ancient Vedic ages tell that:

> They believed in the spirit-world of the *Pitṛ*s or father, where the parted souls go after death. The king or ruler of this place is called Yama. He was the first of the mortals to enter that world and he became the ruler of those who came later. — *Ibid.*: 19

> The Hindus believe that heaven is a realm where the departed souls go to reap the pleasant effects of their good and virtuous actions and they remain there for sometime — that is, until the result of their good work is completely reaped: then after that period, they will return to this world again. — *Ibid.*: 19-20

The Hindus do not believe in the destruction or annihilation by death, but accept disintegration. Rather, it is a mare change of body or form. It means that this "instrument" (body) which had served its purpose so far should be thrown away so that other instrument should be rebuilt. Thus, Vedānta observes that when a person dies, he is not "really dead." Death means just a change from one state of consciousness to another state of consciousness. A soul throws away the gross physical body at the time of death just as a person throws away a worn-out old garment (*Ibid.*: 38). It has a *śloka* (II.22) bearing with

Bhagavad-Gītā:

वासांसि जीर्णानि यथा विहाय
नवानि गृह्णाति नरोऽपराणि।
तथा शरीराणि विहाय जीर्णा-
न्यन्यानि संयाति नवानि देही॥

It is interesting that:

> As we survive and retain our individuality after each seven years of change and renewal, so we live as individual souls after the final dissolution of the form of our bodies.

Every particle of the body changes but in spite of the fact the person continues to exist and this continuity is not broken. This *śloka* (II.13) of *Bhagavad-Gītā* read as under:

देहिनोऽस्मिन् यथा देहे कौमारं यौवनं जरा।
तथा देहान्तर प्राप्ति धीरस्तत्र न मुह्यति॥

> As during our lifetime we survive the death of the baby body, the young body and the mature body, successively, and retain our individuality, so after the death of the old body we shall survive, live, retain our individuality and continue to exist through eternity. — *Ibid.*: 22

In this context two more *śloka*s (II.20 and 23) of *Bhagavad-Gītā* may be mentioned:

न जायते म्रियते वा कदाचि-
न्नायं भूत्वा भविता वा न भूयः।
अजो नित्यः शाश्वतोऽयं पुराणो
न हन्यते हन्यमाने शरीरे॥

> He is not born nor doth he die; nor having been ceaseth he any more to be: unborn, perpetual, eternal and ancient, he is not slain when the body is slaughtered. (Annie Besant, 1998).

नैनं छिन्दन्ति शस्त्राणि नैनं दहति पावकः।
न चैनं क्लेदयन्त्यापो न शोषयति मारुतः॥

> Weapons cleave him not, nor fire burneth him,
> nor water wet him, nor wind drieth him away.

Guidance at Time of Death

Every culture has its own eschatology bearing with death rituals, customs, beliefs and values. But it is interesting that a few societies have specialized areas in which an institution offers "trustworthy guidance" at the time of death and the after-death state into which everyone of human kind must inevitably pass through but of which very few of them have enlightened understanding. It is of inestimable value. It has a reference in *The Tibetan Book of the Dead* (or the *Bardo Thödol*) by W.Y. Evans-Wentz which narrates the exploration of man of the Unknown in a manner which is "truely scientific and Yogic." It has a message that "the Art of Dying is quite as important as the Art of Living" (Evans-Wentz, 1973: v-xxxvi) of which "it is the complement and summation: that the future of being is dependent, perhaps entirely, upon a rightly controlled death," and the art of Reincarnation. This book is similar to the *Egyptian Book of the Dead*.

The book teaches that:

> The dying should face death not only calmly and clear-mindedly and heroically but with an intellect rightly trained and rightly directed, mentally transcending, if need be by bodily suffering and informities, as they would be able to do had they practised efficiently during their active lifetime, during the Art of Living, and, when about to die, the Art of Dying.
>
> — *Ibid.*: xiv-v

It has also a reference of Milarepa Tibetan's saintly master of Yoga who earlier had prepared to die under the same traditional conditions.

> Buddhists and Hindus alike believe that the last thought at the moment of death determines the character of the next incarnation. As the *Bardo Thödol* teaches, so have the sages of India long taught, that the thought-process of a dying person should be rightly directed, preferably by the dying person if he or she has been

> initiated or psychologically trained to meet death, or otherwise, by a guru or a friend or relative versed in the science of death.
>
> — *Ibid.*: xviii

This book has several chapters, some of them are — The Importance of Bardo Thödol, The Symbolism, The Esoteric significance of the Forty-Nine days of the Bardo (during and between death and rebirth), The Esoteric significance of the Five Elements, The Wisdom of Teachings, The Death Ceremonies, The Bardo or After-Death State, The Judgement, the Rebirth Doctrine and The Manuscript.

Dr. C.G. Jung, the Freudian Psychoanalyst while commenting upon the *Bardo Thödol,* tells about the "sexual fantasies." This study has three parts — *Chikhai Bardo, Chönyid Bardo* and *Sidpa Bardo*. Dr. Jung tells —

> This is the realm that corresponds to the last and lowest region of the *Bardo,* known as the *Sidpa Bardo,* where the dead man, unable to profit by the teachings of the *Chikhai* and *Chönyid Bardo,* begins to fall a prey to sexual fantasies and is attracted by the vision of mating couples. Eventually he is caught by a womb and born into the earthly world affair. Meanwhile, as one might expect, the Oedipus complex starts functioning. . . . If his *Karma* destines him to be reborn as a man, he will fall in love with his mother-to-be and his father hateful and disgusting. Conversely, the future daughter will be highly attracted by her father-to-be and repelled by her mother. . .
>
> — Evans-Wentz, 1973: xli

Among Hindus there are religious people who regularly practise several types of yogic *sādhanā* all bearing with "self-realization" and they would always strive to achieve the success. They believe that "I am not this body but am the spirit-Soul." *Bhagavad-Gītā* (II.30) tells:

> देही नित्यमवध्योऽयं देहे सर्वस्य भारत।
> तस्मात् सर्वाणि भूतानि न त्वं शोचितुमर्हसि॥
>
> This dweller in the body of everyone is ever invulnerable, O Bharata; therefore thou shouldst not grieve for any creature.

In this background, at the time of death "we have to finish that process of perfection. During our lifetime we have to practise the method of approaching that perfection so that at the time of death, when we have to give up this material body, that perfection can be realized"(Swami Prabhupada, 1997: 20).

There is still another *śloka* of *Bhagavad-Gītā* (VIII.10) as given below:

> प्रयाणकाले मनसाचलेन भक्त्या युक्तो योगबलेन चैव।
> भ्रुवोर्मध्ये प्राणमावेश्य सम्यक् स तं परं पुरुषमुपैति दिव्यम्॥

> One who, at the time of death, fixes his life-air between the eyebrows and in full devotion engages himself in remembering the Supreme Lord, (he) will certainly attain the Supreme Personality of God-head. — *Ibid.*: 21

There are other relevant *śloka*s of the *Bhagavad-Gītā* as well (VIII.11-12, 13, etc.).

Though such practices are related to higher yogic *sādhanā*, everybody cannot do it. That is why there is a traditional and easy approach of remembering the name of God everytime one utters *Oṁ*, *Viṣṇu*, *Nārāyaṇa*, *Rāma*, *Kṛṣṇa*, *Hanumān*, *Durgā*, *Kālī*, etc. If a person continues this practice throughout, he is most likely to utter such sacred names at the time of death and he may get emancipated. Here reference to a *śloka* (VIII.6) of the *Bhagavad-Gītā* would not be out of place:

> यं यं वापि स्मरन् भावं त्यजत्यन्ते कलेबरम्।
> तं तमेवैति कौन्तेय सदा तद्भावभावितः॥

> Whatsoever at the end abandoneth the body, thinking upon any being, to that being only he goeth, O Kaunteya, ever to that conformed in nature.

The last portion of life is more important than the first, because what you are at the end of this life is what you will be at the beginning of the next (Yogananda, 1970: 68).

It was in this background that in traditional context, people preferred the naming of children to the names of God.

Santa Tulsīdās in *Rāmāyaṇa* also refers to the importance of remembering the name of Rāma at the time of death —

जनम जनम मुनि जतन कराही
अन्त काल राम आवत नाही॥

Similarly, there is a phrase —

अन्त भला तो सब भला

Some of the Jains who are deeply religious or saints, make fasting (*upavāsa*) and they gradually stop taking food or water and die. It is a part of a traditional religious norm.

Transmigration and Reincarnation

Transmigration and reincarnation implies that "a soul must go through many lives on the earth plane, as through so many grades in a school, before it 'graduates' to the immortal perfection of God." (Yogananda, 1970: 61)

An individual has to go through a cycle of lives and it has a continuous chain. Such experience in each succeeding life is linked with his actions in the previous ones. In turn, it determines his conduct and experience in future lives (Shivaram, 1971: 3). K.S. Shivaram in his book, *Transmigration of Souls* makes a factual account and faithful compilation of events recounted by Sri Subbaraya Sharma of an old town of Yedathore close to Mysore. Originally this account was in Kannaḍa (*ibid.*).

In a Hindī book, *Punarjanma Kī Satya Kathāyen*, Harimohan Sharma (1973) reports 26 real stories from Delhi, Mathurā, Saharanpur, Baliā, Goa, London, South Africa, Belgium, Turkey, Hollywood, England and the like.

World Unseen as Recorded

There are certain books throughout the world in which people are anxious to contact the soul when it left its body. Some of them have established "communion" with the soul and have narrated the "world unseen." Anthony Borgia had "recorded" two such companion books — *Life in the World Unseen* and *More about Life in the World Unseen* (1956).

The Spirit-communicator of the book was known on earth as Monsignor Robert Hugh Benson who was a son of Edward White Benson, a former Archbishop of Canterbury.

In the scripts that have followed, Benson had dealt with an extensive variety of subjects in connection with the spirit world including "theology," which underwent a wholesale and drastic revision. His main occupation was to meet people at their dissolution and conduct them into the spirit-world. Working with him were his friends, Edwin and Ruth. Some chapters of the second book deal with — A Passing, The Awakening, Spirit Intercourse, Spirit Locomotion, A Lesson in Creation, Philosophers' Folly, The Ruler of the Realms (Borgia, 1956: 7-9).

Spiritual Dimension

For more than a century spiritualism has made considerable development convincing many scientific minds who have been earnestly seeking for the truth of man's survival after death. It started with Experimental Spiritualism in 1870 when in the following year Sir William Crook, a reputed scientist and an extraordinary genius began his investigation with the aid of the "medium," Mrs. Florence Cook (Appendix 1). Crooks' experiment lasted for three years with that celebrated medium.

During this period he took all precautions against all possible fraud or trickery imaginable and he employed scientific methods of observation and experiments with delicate instruments. The seances were held in his own house with honest friends who were equally eager to discover whether there was any truth in the spirit phenomena. Many Americans became familiar with the name of Katie king, the spirit-control of Mrs. Florence Cook. She materialized herself, her pulsations were recorded, her heart-beating was heard, she was photographed and she distributed locks of her materialized hair to those who were present there . . . all these happened under strictly test conditions in his own rooms where electric wires with bells were fixed on the walls, so that the least little intrusion from outside could be instantly detected.

Sir Crook's experiments were at first ridiculed by the scientific world but Sir Crook was committed. He had the courage of his conviction which led him to publish the reports of his experiments and he kept doing so ever since.

Later on, as a number of other eminent persons, including D.D. Home, Edimund Gurmey, Dr. F.W.H. Myers, Frank Podomore, Alfred Russel Wallace, William James, Sir Oliver Lodge, Mr. Thompson, Dr. Hodgeson, C.N. Jones, Camide Flamarion, W.T. Stead, Prof. Hyslop coming from different places like England, London, Harvard, Birmingham, Michigan and the like became interested. Some of these people did scientific spiritual experiments, published relevant books, papers, lectures and established relevant forums or institutions like "Society for the Psychical Research," "American Institute of Scientific Research," "British Assoication," etc.

Although many of the professional mediums have been pitifully exposed as frauds there are however genuine mediums and authentic spirit-manifestations which cannot be explained by telepathy or by any other theory than that of the communication of discarnate spirits. On many occasions the audience is deceived by the earth-bound spirits. The manifestations on the material plane, such as table turning and rapping knocks of the spirit, are ordinarily understood by spiritualism, but all such phenomena belong to a lower class of spiritualism or spiritism as it is called by many. (Abhedananda, 1960:1-5)

There are certain souls who retain their consciousness but they do not know that they are dead. They are in a state of "confusion." They require some time to realize that they are dead. (*ibid.*: 192)

Swami Vivekananda (1955: 26) while referring to F. Schnurrer (*Chronik der Seuchen*, 1825) speaks of a "principle that the numbers of births in a given population has the most decided influence upon the length of life and mortality in it, as this always keeps pace with mortality: so that always and everywhere the deaths and the births increase and decrease in like proportion, which he places beyond doubt by an accumulation of evidence collected from many lands and their various provinces. . . ."

Spiritualism and Spiritism

The "spiritualism" and "spiritism" are derived from the root word "spirit" or "soul" which means "the breath which animates the body and it is its "principle of life."

Spiritualism in many circles and several writings still seems to be a misunderstood term and generally it is confused with spiritism.

> Spiritism . . . may be defined as the belief that it is possible to communicate with the 'spirits' of the dead so as to receive from them intelligent messages and proofs of their identity and survival, and as the study and practice of so doing.
>
> . . . Spiritism naturally has a strong attraction from those who have suffered bereavement, while their sense of loss is poignant; but the spirit-world is also a source of repulsion and an object of dread. . . .
>
> — Hastings, 1920: 805

Abhedananda (1960: 5) tells that

> Spiritism can only satisfy our curiosity and does not explain any of our vital questions. But true spiritualism should be distinguished from that phrase which is called spiritism. Higher spiritualism therefore is the name for that which starting from the belief in a life after death, reveals the nature of the soul and its relation to God. This higher spiritualism is at the root of all great

> religions of the world. Communications with so called angels or messangers of God or *Devas* or bright spirits as they are called in India have been the source of Knowledge and inspiration of the Prophets and Seers of the Old and New Testaments. From the time of Abraham, Jacob and Moses down to the time of Christ and his disciples all Prophets and seers saw the spirits, heard them speak and followed their teachings. . . .

I feel that there is nothing like "lower" or "higher" classes of spiritualism, as Abhedananda has mentioned. Spiritualism is the opposite concept of materialism. A person who is spiritualist, "turns upward" (*ūrdhvadvāra*), the soul gets "spiritual-pull" and subsequently gets "linked-up" with the "Ultimate Supreme Being" which the *Bhagavad-Gītā* in one of the *ślokas* (VI.28) refers to:

> युञ्जन्नेवं सदात्मानं योगी विगतकल्मषः ।
> सुखेन ब्रह्मसंस्पर्शमत्यन्तं सुखमश्नुते ॥

> The sinless *yogī* uniting his self constantly with God easily enjoys the eternal Bliss of oneness with the Brahmā.

Spiritualism is connected with a "spiritual science" which is a "science of consciousness"(*cetana vijñāna*), the apex of it is known as *Brahma-vidyā* otherwise known as *para-vidyā*, *vihaṅgama yoga*, *sahaja yoga*, etc. "Spirituality," though it is allied to "religion," appear to be distinct (Sahay, 1998: 29, 113, 223; 1999: 194). *Brahma-vidyā* sprang up from Brahmā (Supreme Being or *para Brahman* itself). *Brahma-vidyā* has two parts (1) *bāhya tattva-jñāna* (outer knowledge of elements through texts): and (2) *abhyantara bheda sādhanā* (inmost mystic spiritual practice). Once a person who is adept, of course it is rare, the person gets almost every knowledge in the earth or the *brahmāṇḍa* (universe), if at all he has to concentrate on the lesser priorities. A spiritualist may casually look into the spiritism, but it is more involved with the real *yoga* which unites the *atmā* with the *parmātmā* (Sahay, 1999: 194).

Scientific Dimension

> Anyone who asserts in the name of Science that there is no life after death, therefore, makes a very unscientific statement. Merely on the basis of scientific knowledge we can neither affirm that there is a life after death nor deny it. . . . The question is beyond its jurisdiction. — Abul A'La Maududi, 1979: 3

In the last several decades scientific researches have brought many truth and relevant laws which were so far unknown to different scriptures of the world.

> They try to explain that when the vital parts of the body wear out in this machine, then naturally the whole of the machine must stop. The vital parts are regarded as the heart, the lungs and the brain. . . . — Abhedananda, 1960: 25

But the pertinent question that arises is "Does the death of the conscious life imply the death of the life of the organs? . . . On the contrary science tells us that the organs do not die immediately after the death of the body or the conscious life." In this context, Rockefeller Institute tells that "there is a heart of a chicken that has been kept for eight years, and it is still going, doing normal action." (*ibid.*: 26) Sri Sri Paramahansa Yogananda entered *mahāsamādhi* in Los Angeles on 7 March 1952.

> The absence of any visual signs of decay in the dead body of Paramahansa Yogananda offers the most extraordinary cases in our experience. . . . No physical disintegration was visible in his body even twenty days after death. . . .
>
> — Yogananda Paramahansa, 1951

Another well-known example was the body of St. Xavier in Goa where the body was kept almost intact for a number of years. So it tells that "the organs have their independent life which may continue to live even after the conscious life of the individual is dead." So modern science tells us that "there are two kinds of death — One is the death of the conscious life (clinical death); the other is the death of the organic and cellular life, which is called somatic life. One does not depend upon the other." (*ibid.*: 26)

Materialistic science does not give a clear idea of what death really means though science goes on trying to trace the cause of death and describes the signs of death. "Science tells us that the actual signs of death are very difficult to find." It tells that "the decomposition and putrefaction are the only final signs of death, and nothing else." Unfortunately, "there have been many cases of premature burial recorded in the medical journals of the world." That is why a premature burial as well as embalming are objectionable (*ibid.*: 27-28).

In this context, trance, catalepsy, ecstasy or *samādhi* are conditions which resemble death. "The outward signs are similar. But what happens to the soul? Science does not know, because it denies the existence of a soul." There are also cases of counterfeits of death even in the lower animals (*ibid.*: 28-31).

In course of trance and others as given above, soul leaves the body, but the connection is not entirely cut off. It still has some kind of connection.

> It is like the umbilical cord of a new born babe which holds this entity as connected with the physical body. Therefore the physical body can be revived: but when the connection is entirely cut off, the body cannot be revived. Then it is called death. That is the difference. This difference very few people understand.
>
> — *Ibid.*: 33

T. Lobsang Rampa (1965) was originally a Tibetan but when his soul was going to leave his body, he took over the body of a Londoner who also was going to die. He managed to take over this new body. Later on he narrated a number of "previous life" and published a number of interesting books. One of them is *You Forever* (1965). This book gives the details of the "Astral-travel" in which the subtle body goes out and is apparently or temporarily "dead." This soul (double) comes out from the body through "silver cord" and floats to different places as he or she wishes. This soul is invisible. In this book Rampa gives 30 lessons for the Astral-travel and it has also a few sketches.

Ectoplasm and Photography

It is interesting that when the living soul goes out of the body during death, it can be photographed. This instrument is most delicate and sensitive. It has been used to weigh the body, just before death and immediately after death. It constitutes the "finer substance" which has a definite weight of about half an ounce or three-quarter of an ounce. This fine substance which emanates from the dying body has a luminosity and it has been photographed. It can be seen by the psychic. The whole body becomes enshrouded with a kind of "luminous mist" (Abhedananda, 1960: 33).

Scientists have taken up that subject in Europe and are experimenting on this emanation. They call it *ectoplasm* (Appendix 2). It is a vapour like substance. But it has no particular form. It is like a cloud, but it can take a shape or a form, and can be photographed. What substance it is, they do not know; but they cannot deny its existence (*ibid.*).

> Our human bodies are emanating that substance all the time. It can be seen especially at the time when there is a medium in a trance-like condition. The materializing mediums emanate that very strongly. I have seen it in seances, and in private seances when there was no professional medium at all. I have handled it, touched it. There is no particular feeling when we feel *ectoplasm*. It cannot be described. But when it takes a definite shape then it becomes almost like solid, like flesh of our own body. It can take any form. — *Ibid.*: 33-34

During death all vital forces of the body which are governing the different organs, become concentrated and centralized into one point.

> The dying person's sight becomes dim, and the sensations of the body becomes faint, and gradually the whole body is going through a transformation. . . . Some of the dying persons develop

> clairvoyance and clairaudience. They can appear just at the time of death, either before or immediately after, to distant friends, in the form of an apparition, and they can give their messages. Such cases have been recorded by the scientists.
>
> This *ectoplasm* is a substance which contains finer matter in vibration, and finer matter forms the undergarment of the soul, and the gross physical body is the outer garment. So, we have two bodies, the gross physical body and the finer or ethereal body, which exists in each one of us. — *Ibid.*: 34

The ethereal body which contains ectoplasm "cannot be seen until it is brought within the range of our vision by a process which is called materialization . . ." Vedānta refers to "subtle body" (*sūkṣmaśarīram*) which is the undergarment of the soul, and the gross physical body is the outer garment (*ibid.*: 35).

Taittirīya Upaniṣad tells us that the soul in man is screened by five covering bodies called as *pañca koṣa* (five sheaths). The outermost is the Gross body which is nourished by food (*anna*) known as *annamaya koṣa*. The four other *koṣa*s are "Ethereal body," "Astral body," "Bauddhic body" and "Cosmic body" respectively (Sahay, 1998: 84).

The body is the instrument through which the soul must manifest its powers, gain experiences, learn the lessons and gather knowledge. In this way, the living soul is progressing in the process of evolution, rising from a lower to a higher state and fulfilling its mission and every step of manifestation (*ibid*: 36).

Ancestors and Social System

A person who had kinsman and deeply involved in loving relations with them for a number of years if dies, such relationship is not abruptly snapped. It continues of course on a different dimension all coming under the social system of a society which has a network of varied dyadic relation with different roles and norms connected with responsibilities and expectations (Radcliffe-Brown, 1994: 194). It is the similar type of relationship that a person has with Gods or deities. The person who is deceased, is believed to acquire some sort of "supernatural power" and help the relatives or kinsmen. As it is a supernatural entity, "fear" and "reverence" get combined together. So, this situation leads to worship of the ancestors (*pitṛ*s or *pitṛloka*). But it is a both-way process. The kinsmen respect, give offerings to the ancestors during birth, marriage, agricultural activities, festivals or the whole life-cycle rituals or calamities and the like. In turn, the ancestors give blessings, prosperity and protect misfortunes of the family.

Ancestor-worship is one of the earliest forms known in the society though they are not universal. Where a man dies, varying societies — may be tribals, non-tribals and urbanites — undergo elaborate rituals, normally known as *śrāddha* (death ritual).

Hindus have a series of elaborate death-rituals covering. *dhārmika* as well as *laukika* aspects. For the eleven days, the soul of the dead hovers in the house but after the performance of rituals by the *paṇḍita*, the soul goes to the proper place. People who are well off, very religious or if a spirit (soul) has some problems, they propitiate and pray to the *pitṛ*s to bless them and pray to the souls to alleviate their sufferings in this world. Many of them go to the famous pilgrim places like, Gayā and get the elaborate *śrāddha* conducted during the occasion of *pitṛ-pakṣa* (*mahālaya*). In the home also the eldest son whose father is dead, performs *tarpaṇa* (water-oblation) during *mahālaya*. It is a pious duty for the son and unless he does it, the *pitṛ*s are said to be in distress for want of food in the other world and if the *pitṛ*s are annoyed, they go to the extent of cursing. There is also the provision of annual *śraddha* which is known as *barkhī* (*barsī*). During *śrāddha*, among the many rituals, there are *pitṛmilāonī* in which the spirit gets ritually affiliated with the *pitṛloka*s, and *śayyādāna* which is offered to the officiating *paṇḍita* on behalf of the dead-spirit so that it becomes comfortable.

In Bihar, traditionally, the village people have *śira-ghara* or *kula-devatā-ghara* or *gosāin-ghara* housed in the seniormost family of the lineage. In association with other regional or local deities, they install the ancestors (*kula-devatā)* in the ancestral house. The *kula-devatā*s protect and help the family or lineage-members. Reciprocally, its members placate and offer various food items and other necessary articles to the *kula-devatā*s. The *kula-devatā*s of *śira-ghara* also include those who after death became ghosts, appear as apparition, disturb the family or they appear in dreams and want to have appeasements. As such, these spirits are "ritually fixed" and given a specific place among the ancestors by a symbolic *piṇḍa* (small heap of earth) on the floor over a wooden-plank (*śira-pīḍhā*), *tikka* (small lines or round adorning marks of vermillion) or on a niche (recess in a wall) (Sahay, 2001: 240). Clothes, specific food and *pakavāna* are offered to the ancestors during birth, *muṇḍana*, marriage and also on festivals (*ibid*.: 317). During marriage a woman makes a *pitar-neotā* and respectfully invites all the revered *pitar*s (ancestors) for the marriage. It starts from the oldest known dead generation serially and genealogically in a descending order. On this occasion, hand-written invitation-letter containing betel-nuts are presented to the ancestors in the *śira-ghara* (*ibid*.: 207-8).

Ancestor-worship is prevalent among many tribals of the country. It has been a common practice, though varying in rituals, among the tribals of undivided Bihar. These tribals believe that "dead ancestors were the real benefactors of the families or the group to which they belonged, and that they are easily approachable by their living kinsmen." They invoke their ancestors on important occasions of their life, whether it is birth, marriage, death, festivals, as also during calamity. Some people pour a few drops of liquor on the ground in the name of ancestors before they drink. Even the first fruits of their fields are offered to ancestors. According to the Sauria and Mal Paharia, "death is not the complete negation of life but it is a resurrection which envisages life after death." These tribals believe that their ancestors always remain with them and help them. "On all occasions, birth, marriage, death, also at the harvesting of each crop, season-wise and crop-wise, the hosts of spirits along with the ancestors are worshipped and offered 'Puja'." (Prasad, 1961: 282)

Immortality?

On few occasions I had the opportunity to join the death-procession of a celebrity who had immensely contributed to the society. In such procession some would make loud slogans — "this person is immortal" (*ve amara rahen*). Besides, such other persons who were professors, doctors, engineers, industrialists, scientists, artists, soldiers, social-workers, administrators, nationalists or persons of eminence in other various walks of life, coming from local, regional and national level, had left the footprints. People never forget their invaluable contributions to the society and feel highly indebted. To perpetuate the memory of such persons, a number of things are done — hanging the photo-frames of the person on different places, naming the house, organization, roads, *mohallā*, market places, trophy, station, parks and the like.

Even if the deceased is an ordinary person, the family in its own way try to perpetuate the memory. The progeny itself is a reflection of the elders, generally considered to be the "chip of the old block," may be on the level of physical or mental traits, or the heritage.

Dissolution of an organism means "death." It is "mortal." Its opposite is known as "immortality." In this context, broadly speaking, we find that there are three important interrelated aspects or terms of reference. The first one is the "physical." The "physical form" of the body gets dissolved at the time of death, and "this form" never comes again. It is this aspect which we call "mortal". The second aspect is "spiritual." A person has two things — the "body" and the "soul." Even though the person is dead, the other part, i.e., the "soul" or "subtle body" — covered under the *pañca koṣa* — gets transformed, and this part is "not mortal," i.e., "immortal." It continues through transmigration and rebirth till the favourable condition evolves and finally gets salvation. A number of *ślokas* of *Bhagavad-Gītā* confirm it. The third aspect is "social." A person who lives in the society is evaluated on the basis of his works. If he had helped and contributed to the society, people will remember him, even after his death, and will keep him *alive* in their memory. "They won't allow him to *die* and as such he becomes immortal."

Cosmology has a number of components with innumerable animate and inanimate things. The whole cosmic system governs a series of scientific as well as mystic laws by the Supreme Creator. It is highly functional, and each of it has the meaning and explanation, even though man has the serious limitations to conceive, define or communi-cate with others. It starts with birth and journeys through young age, adulthood, marriage, old age, death and beyond it; but again it comes back to birth, covering all in its own small sub-system within the grand cosmic system.

The solar system of the celestial bodies, connected with the earth, works in a circle. So is the case with the life-cycle of the human being and also of the smallest molecule. Is it not a mystery? In this background, if we look into the grand cosmic system and the sub-systems of the Universe, the questions regarding the death of a person and mortality get lost. Within the grand cosmic system each of the components, including human beings, is desired by the "cosmic sports" (*līlā*) to contribute duties and accomplish responsibilities appropriately.

If the soul, which houses a person, is spiritually evolved and gets elevated, it overweighs the physical death. Even in the social world such persons become immortal.

Conclusion

The study of life beyond death, as discussed above, is relevant but it won't be complete unless the "purpose" of the study gets delineated. Such study is all the more important since we are fast passing through the valuable *karmayoni* and the life may get terminated any time.

Everybody wants to know what happens to the life after death. It is a natural curiosity exending from a casual information to obsession. If it starts from a philosophical or thelogical question, it turns into the dimension of occult phenomenon, and becomes a mystery. However, it must be satisfactory also from intellectual or cognitive point of view.

Curiosity is not enough. It is a vital question having bearing with the past life and actions. Logically, the present life should be spent so judiciously, so that the future life would be much better. It has a bearing with the "everyday life" and the moral aspects of what is *good* (positive) and what is *bad* (negative) in the society. One has to render accounts of one's own conduct followed by another life.

One should develop a "philosophy of life," a proper awareness and attitude. "Pleasure" and "enjoyment" in life may be good, but one should also appreciate that there is a difference between *preya* and *śreya*. *Kaṭhopaniṣad* tells that *śreya* is the excellent path of true welfare. Even though one takes the responsibilities of the chores of daily life, as a *gr̥hastha*, one should also develop another dimension of life which is "self- realization," and pose certain questions — Who am I?, What is the main purpose of life?, What I can "carry" after death? Mundanity and spirituality are two different dimensions in life, both are necessary. They should be combined and have proper coordinations till that stage of life when spirituality takes over the mundanity.

Another relevant point which emerges out of it is the "entry-points of spiritualism." Of course, it is of universal importance. There may be several such entry-points (spiritual attributes), but at the moment we may refer to only seven of them, viz., Theism (functional), Purity, Temperance, Love to all Beings, Charity, Honesty and Discipline. Each of the positive attributes is considered to be potential. It is functional, and it leads to other higher positive attributes as well. If it is given proper importance, the person becomes elevated and spiritual, even in the "next birth."

One of the famous *śloka*s (II.14) of *Bhagavad-Gītā* tells that "your right is to work only, but never to the fruit thereof. Be not instrumental in making your actions bear fruit, not let your attachment to be to the action." There are people who argue on this. Others just agree with it. The third category of people could use it sincerely, only when they are exposed to the spiritual surroundings.

There are different *yoga sādhanā* (spiritual practice) as given in scriptures, disseminating the "functional knowledge" through different *sant*s or spiritual adepts. Under the circumstances when such people start the spiritual practice, their "consciousness goes upward" (*ūrdhvadhara*) in this and the "next life."

Even at the time of vital death, as *Bhagavad-Gītā* (VIII.10) tells, if a person fixes his breath between the eyebrows and in full devotion engages himself in remembering the Supreme Lord, he will certainly reach Him.

As mentioned earlier, one's relationship with one's kinsmen is not abruptly snapped after his physical death. In fact he becomes an ancestor (*pitṛ*) and continues to live in various dimensions, all coming under the social system. These dimensions — spiritual and social — hold importance, and if the person elevates himself and immensely contributes to the society, he becomes virtually immortal. It is a both-way process. The person gives respect and offerings to the ancestor. On the other hand, the ancestor gives blessings and prosperity to the whole family.

References

Abhedananda, Swami, 1960, *Life Beyond Death*, Abhedananda Memorial Series no.1, Ramkrishna Math, Calcutta.

Besant, Annie 1998, *The Bhagavad-Gītā*, The Theosophical Publishing House, Chennai.

Bhaktivedanta, Swami A.C. Prabhupada, 1997, *Beyond Birth and Death*, The Bhaktivedanta Book Trust, Mumbai.

Borgia, Anthony, 1956, *More About Life in the World Unseen*, Recorded, Odhams Press Limited, Long Acre, London.

Evans-Wentz, W.Y., 1973, *The Tibetan Book of the Dead*, Compiled and Edited, Oxford University Press, New York.

Hastings, James, 1920, (ed.), *Encyclopaedia of Religion and Ethics*, vol. X, Edinburg.

Jung, C.G., 1973, "Psychological Commentary," In *Tibetan Book of the Dead*, Compiled and Edited, Oxford University Press, New York.

King, James, 1816, *The Holy Bible*, King James Version, American Bible Society, New York.

Mandrelle, J.P.G., 1995, *Facing Death*, Secretary, North Indian Christian Trust & Book Society, Allahabad.

Maududi, Abul A'La, 1979, *Life After Death*, Markazi Makhtaba Islamia, Delhi.

Nikhilananda, Swami, 1949, *The Upaniṣads* (*Kaṭha Upaniṣad*), vol. 1, Bonaza Book, New York.

Prasad, N., 1961, *Land and People of Tribal Bihar*, Bihar Tribal Research Institute, Ranchi.

Radcliffe-Brown, A.R., 1994, *Structure and Function in Primitive Society*, Cohen & West Ltd., London.

Rampa, T., Lobsang, 1965, *You Forever*, Corgi Books Transworld Publishing Ltd., London.

Sahay, K.N., 1976, *Under the Shadow of the Cross*, Institute of Social Research and Applied Anthropology, Calcutta.

———, 1998, *Spiritual Anthropology*, Commonwealth Publishers, New Delhi.

———, 1999, *Beyond The Thousand Petalled Lotus and the Science of Consciousness*, Commonwealth Publishers, New Delhi.

———, 2001, *Ambastha Kayastha* (*The Evolution of a Family and Its Socio-Cultural Dimension*), Commonwealth Publishers, New Delhi.

Sharma, Harimohan, 1973, *Punarjanm Kī Satya Kathāyen* (Hindi), Hind Books Limited, Delhi.

Shivaram, K.S., 1971, *Transmigration of Souls* (*Pre-Existence and Rebirth*), A Factual Account, 35, Sampige Road, Malleswaram, Bangalore.

Tiwari, Kedar Nath, 1983, *Comparative Religion*, Motilal Banarsidass, Patna.

Vivekananda, Swami, 1955, *Life After Death*, Advaita Ashrama, Calcutta.

Yogananda, Paramahansa, 1951, *Autobiography of a Yogi*, Dakshineshwar, Jaico Publishing House, Bombay.

———, 1970, *The Mystery of Life and Death & Other Lectures*, Yogoda Math, Dakshineshwar, Calcutta.

Appendix I

The Medium and the Spirit
(Prof. Crooks is showing that the Medium and the Spirit are different from each other)
Painted by S. Drixin

Appendix II

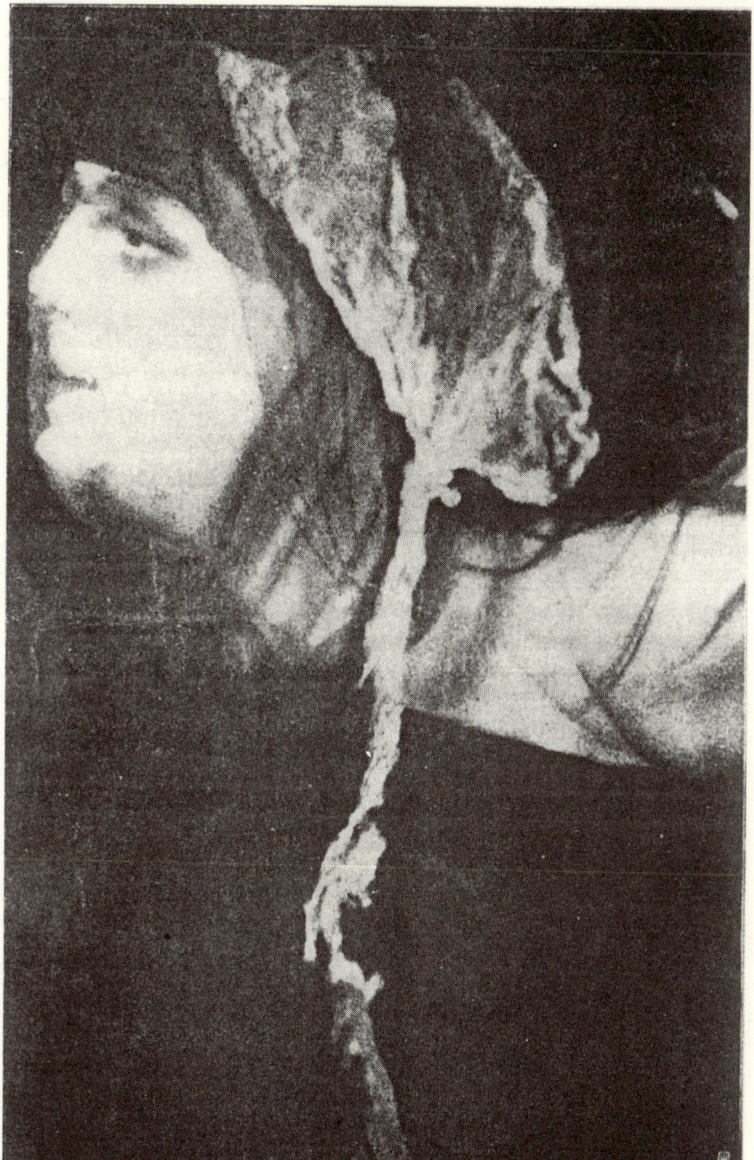

The face of the Spirit has been materialized, with the help of the Octoplasm of the Medium.

4

Death in Liṅgāyatism

K.G. Gurumurthy

DEATH as a phenomenon haunts all conscious human beings in different ways irrespective of their faiths. It is said that birth is a chance and death is certain. But this statement is not true in all religious traditions since there are a few religions which neither believe in certainty of death nor the uncertainty of birth. The believers further differ whether death is final or is there any rebirth and life after death. Those who believe that death is an end in itself form one group, others who believe in life after death form another. There are still others who believe that "death" is temporary and end of only the present birth. In this sense, death also means the beginning of another birth. Similarly a few religious traditions believe that life on earth is hard and full of agony and suffering, and death is its only solution. Further-more, those who believe in rebirth necessarily believe in the existence of soul and different worlds — heaven above, hell below and the earthly world in the middle. According to them, soul is subject to rewards and punishments in heaven and hell, for its good and bad deeds on earth. Thus in these religious traditions, as an individual gets old he is naturally haunted by death.

The theological matters such as: "whether soul carries the load of merits and demerits (*pāpa* and *puṇya*) to the next birth, is there a soul, whether it is a part of god or not and the purpose of its coming to and going from earth?" are important. Though there is no one explanation for these, all believe in the presence of something super biological in man. Why a soul aspires to take a rebirth is another question. For example, Hindus believe that when a soul intends to redeem its demerits (*karma*) and collect merit to relieve itself from the cycle of births and deaths, it has to take birth first on earth, may be in the form of a lower animal. Later on as it goes on earning merit in each rebirth, it gets the human form. They also believe that after several crores of deaths and rebirths (*punarapi jananam, punarapi maraṇam*) a soul gets this form. Hindus further believe that it is only through human form that salvation is possible, because it is only man who is blessed with consciousness (*chetana*) to distinguish the good from bad. So he should make use of this chance properly and help the soul to get salvation. If it fails it will not only lose its chance to go to heaven but will also be punished by being condemned to hell, where most severe punishments are given. Furthermore it will be ordered to begin the birth-death cycle again from the lowest animal form.

The religions, which believe in more than one world, also arrange them in a hierarchy on the basis of the facilities available there. For example, heaven is associated with good, and hell with bad. Depending upon its merits, a soul is sent to one of these stations, or one after another. The length of its stay there again depends upon the balance it has earned on earth.

Religious traditions can also be grouped into those belonging to biological, socio-cultural or philosophical levels on the basis of levels or rewards given to them. Hindu scriptures tell that heaven is a cool and green place with plenty of delicious food and drinks and one need not have to work there for a living. Above all, he will be in the company of heavenly beauties. On the other hand, in hell, one has to work hard and also undergo punishment. These include pain to the body by starvation and thirst, beating, slashing, splitting, branding and dipping into hot and cold fluids, and so on. As we can notice, in both these worlds, it is only the body that is well or ill treated and not the soul. On the basis of these explanations given, we can classify such religions under the biological category. The religions, which have ways and means to "treat" the soul, come under the non-biological category. For example, a soul getting salvation in the Vedic tradition comes under this category.

Religious traditions can also be classified on the basis of how they treat dead and death, either as a temporary phenomenon or permanent. Zoroastrians, Sūfīs and Vīraśaivas treat death as a temporary phenomenon, caused by an act of some evil forces. Once this passes, the "dead" raises again in the name of resurrection. This person is now believed to have more powers, which can be used for societal good. The good examples are Jesus Christ and Sūfī saints. Hence, their corpse is preserved in a tomb-chamber. Others who do not have such belief dispose off the corpse by cremating it, putting it on the Mercy Tower or cutting and feeding it to birds.

Ritual traditions are also classified into classical and Protestant religions. The former are orthodox, traditional, ritualistic, text-based priest-oriented and institution-centred. They are exploitative, opposing change in religious as well as societal spheres. They advocate for one supreme God, patriarchal society and estate-holding systems with concentration of ritual, political and monetary powers in one centre. They fight fearlessly to retain these with them. They not only oppose attempts to bring change (Srinivas 1952, 1956) but also suppress them, often using force. For this, in the past, they used the ruler of the land and sacred texts. Even gods are not spared and they are used in the name of incarnation. However, such autocratic religions meet equally powerful opposition and, as a result, all religions have become protesters. Catholicism, Brāhamaṇical Hinduism and such other religions fall into this category.

The sects found in many religions today are the result of such conflict in them. The good examples are the Catholics and Protestants among the Christians; Shiyas and Sunnis among the Muslims; Śaivites and Vaiṣṇavites among the

Hindus; Mahāyāna and Hīnayāna among the Buddhists; Digambara and Śvetāmbara among the Jains; Bonpo and Zeans among the Taoists; and so on.

Protest Religions

A study of protest, also known as civil religions, reveals that they emerged to lodge their protest against the rigid, exploitative religious practices. To begin with, the protest was against priestly groups who enjoyed maximum benefits and influence over the masses and kings alike in the name of religion. To gain these they often replaced reasoning with myths, miracles and blind beliefs. They had also told that all occurrences in nature are sent by the god, as rewards or punishments. To gain momentum for their arguments both groups started collecting supporters. Even the ruler of the land aligned or embraced the dominant religion of the land since his success depended on the support of his subjects. (Aśoka of Magadha, the Rāyas of Vijayanagara and the Hoysalas of Dvārasamudra had done this). Had they not done this, their dissidents would have supported the enemy during the invasion from outside which would have led to the downfall of not only the king but also their religion. This would also have resulted in the revival of the earlier religious tradition of the land.

Thus, throughout the world and all along the history, kings and religious leaders teamed up to gain control over the masses. As a result protestors continued to exist, though not all of them survived for long since many of them did not have a solid ideological base. Secondly, when the protestors pointed out the drawbacks in the practices of the existing religion, the latter readily accepted and compromised with them. But gradually they went back to the old ways, which were textual. Sanskritization, Islamization and Christianization are good examples of these.

Liṅgāyatism: Origin and Organization

Liṅgāyatism, a protest-religion of Hinduism, came into

existence during the twelfth century, in south India. Its founder was Bāsavannā (1105-67AD), a Telugu Śaiva brāhmaṇa by birth. Right from his childhood, he had noticed a number of gender and birth discriminations and exploitations going on in the name of religion. He often questioned his elders as to why education facilities, thread-ceremony, remarriage and temple entry are open only to a selected few. When he himself was asked to undergo the thread-ceremony, he refused it and also left his home in search of answers to his questions.

After many months of wandering, during 1121AD, he found his preceptor — Īśa Paṇḍita, who had his hermitage school on the confluence of rivers Kṛṣṇā and the Malaprabha called Saṅgama. When he was in his fifth year of schooling his father — a super *mahājan* of an Agrahāra by name Bagevāḍī, died and Bāsava was called back to shoulder the family responsibilities. After attending the funerary rites he however gifted all his properties and left Bagevāḍī with his widowed sister and mother to his maternal grandmother's place. Leaving them there, he returned to Saṅgama to continue his studies and stayed there for another seven years.

During his twelve long years' stay with his teacher, Bāsavannā had earned proficiency in Vedic, Āgamic and Purāṇic literature. He also got his doubts pertaining to Hindu religion and society of his time, their structure, organization, strength and weakness clarified. He learnt the history of protest-religions of India such as Jainism and Buddhism, and their drawbacks and inabilities to fight Hinduism since these religious ideologies themselves had accepted gender discrimination, glorification of celibacy and asceticism, and they had showed least concern for common man. So he designed plans for the establishment of a universal, humanitarian religion, which can thoroughly change the hierarchical and inegalitarian Hindu society. As Ishwaran puts it:

> He worked out the components, the whole structure of such a society and the strategy for its realization. He saw to it that this ideal society and also the strategy are founded on the principle of

> cooperation between equals. It was a society, which had no room for the brāhmaṇas or the untouchables (*Holeya*), no place for gender-discrimination, no scope for occupational hierarchy. He believed that every individual should pursue an occupation of his choice while respecting the occupations of the other. Everyone should live by this sweat and labour but hand over to the community any surplus beyond what was necessary for his household survival.

In 1132 AD, when Bāsavannā was 28 years old, he came to Maṅgalavāḍe, a principality ruled by Bijjala II, belonging to Kalcūri dynasty. One of his uncles worked in the king's court, who helped him to get a job there. During 1132-53 AD Bāsavannā had made considerable progress both as an official and founder of the Liṅgāyat religion. After the death of his uncle, he was elevated to the post held by him and later Bāsavannā was appointed as the minister in charge of finance.

On the religious side he could identify a group of like-minded people such as Allama, Channabasavannā, Siddarāma, Māchideva, Āyadakki Mārayya and his wife, Moolige Mārayya and his wife, Chandayya, Cowdayya, Gattiwālayya and Nilammā who got attracted to Maṅgalavāḍe. In 1141, he could also establish the hall of Śiva experience, a type of religious parliament (*anubhavamaṇḍapa*). Here matters pertaining to the new religion were freely discussed by one and all. The discussions were so free and varied that they attracted a large number of people from all over India. Initially, these meetings were held in the house of Bāsavannā under his chairmanship. When the attendance grew in number and the meetings prolonged, they were shifted to a separate and bigger hall. Bāsavannā, who was a minister in the king's court, could not find enough time to chair these meetings. So Allamā was appointed as its chairman. He was a theological visionary by his own right. Under his chairmanship the topics and discussions were directed towards a doctrinal clarification and consolidation of the programme for organizing and developing a Liṅgāyat community. Each day was set apart for a set of them and the Śiva Śaraṇas came there with thoughts formally written out.

> Sometimes oral presentation was first made and then the thoughts were committed to writing. Most of this literature dealt with the problems of systematizing the institutional and ideolgical structures necessary for constructing a Liṅgāyat community.
>
> — Ishwaran, 1992: 72

Bāsavannā realized that all the religions in India of his time were creating fear among the devotees and exploiting them. So he decided to establish a religion with democratic ideals where there would be no room for ignorance, exploitation, discrimination, forming religious institutions such as temples and *maṭhas*, and priests. In this context, the individual could personally attend to his religious needs by worshipping the personal emblem of Śiva, *Iṣṭaliṅga*. He realized that celibacy and asceticism are against nature and society, and hence disapproved them and upheld householder's life instead. He had also learnt that majority of the people in the society were either of worldly or non-worldly nature (*pravṛt* or *nivṛt*) and most of their energy, knowledge and wealth were wasted on pleasure-seeking and on rites and rituals, and very little was spent on the development of the society. He had also realized that the sacredness attributed to the Sanskrit language, in which most of the Hindu texts were written, had come in the way of dissemination of religious knowledge to the general masses. Hence he decided to give his message in the local language — Kannaḍa — and in the form of simple poems — *vacanas*.[1]

---

1. *Vacana* are small poems of 4-5 lines and written in simple Kannaḍa language. They are loaded with devotion and wisdom. About seventeen thousand of them written by different Śaraṇas are available so far. The idea of conveying religious teachings in simple words and in the language of the masses, i.e., outside Sanskrit is not new to India. Centuries earlier the Buddhists had used Pāli and Prākṛt, Māgadhī and *Jātaka* tales to spread the teachings of Buddha. The *vacanas* are as simple as the one given below:

   Steal not, kill not, and lie not
   Never lose the temper, feel no disgust at others
   Indulge not in self-adulation, speak not ill of others

→

Bāsavannā also wanted to do away with blind beliefs and flying faiths. In one of his *vacanas*, he brushed aside the four thousand years of established Hindu religious tradition and the great epics by questioning the story of Karṇa in the *Mahābhārata* with the words "Is it ever possible to be born through an ear." By this he wanted to do away with the blind beliefs propagated by the epics. In another *vacanas* he tells that birth alone is not the criterion to follow certain occupations.[2] He was in favour of achieved status and wanted to do away with birth as the basis of individual's status. With this he intended to do away with the four-fold division of the Hindu society prescribed under the *varṇa dharma*. He told that dedication to work (*kāyaka*) rather than the ritual clealiness should be the notion attached to occupation (Ramakrishna, 2000). Bāsavannā told that vocation (labour) should be perceived with service-mindedness (*dāsoha*) and like worship (*kāyave kailāsa*). He wanted to bring gender equality and so rejected the impor-tance given to the five types of high level ritual pollutions attributed by the Hindu sacred texts.[3] By

→ This is inner purification, this is outward cleanliness
This is, indeed, the way to win
Our Kudalasangamadeva's pleasure!

2. The Liṅgāyats do not discriminate on the basis of birth or occupation and firmly believe in the commitment and devotion to work. Here is a *vacana* of Bāsava to support this belief:

   You are a blacksmith if you heat:
   A washerman if you beat;
   A weaver, if you lay the warp;
   A Brahmin, if you read the Books!
   Is anybody in the world
   Delivered through the ear?
   Therefore, O Kudala Sangama Lord,
   The well-born is the man who knows
   The nature of Divinity!

3. The Liṅgāyats also do not practice any gender discrimination regarding the status, roles, work allotment and religious duties. They hold that man is a product of nature and he or she has to be accepted in this sense and not with any colour. In one of his *vacanas* Devara Dasinmayya says:

→

rejecting the *varṇāśrama dharma* — four-stage of life perceived in Hinduism — Bāsavannā wanted to do away with the Brāhmaṇical way of institutionalized learning in sectarian schools (*gurukula*), under a religious teacher who gave knowledge in the form of "blessings." Here education was imparted mechanically by rote, repeating the text, like a parrot. The Śaraṇas have compared this type of education to food carried in a packet for the belly.[4] Education suggested by the Śaraṇas was for change. He rejected the earlier notion of education, which was given to uphold, protect and perpetuate the Sanskritic religion and existing the social order.

Bāsavannā also wanted to make religion a mass movement and to achieve this he founded the religious parliament. Till the Śaraṇas came on the scene, the religious matters were considered sacred, confined to the high born and learned. Contrary to this, the discussions transpired in this hall were

---

→ If breasts appear, they say female
If beard and mustache appear, they say male
How about the soul within them? Male or female?

4. This is compared better in the following *vacana*s by Bāsavannā and Siddarāma:

    What's true wisdom, indeed?
    Not learning the Gita by rote
    Not chanting the Vedas complete;
    It's being more than knowing;
    It's great trust in god;
    It's an active career of service;
    It's courage in the face of death
    O Lord, Kudala Sangama!

    Siddarāma, another Śaraṇa, who was also one of the members of the hall of religious parliament, says, that god is pleased by total devotion to him and not by the chanting of Vedas or burning of incense articles. He says in the following words:

    You are no lover of the Vedas
    You are no lover of scriptures
    You are no lover of hymns of praise
    You are no lover of spiritual liberation
    I believe you to be a lover of devotion
    And took refuge in you;
    Save me Kapilasiddamallikarjuna.

neither discourses nor sermons, and never directed by a religious head but only moderated by a chairman, Allamā, who was a householder and a musical drummer in a temple by profession. Till then such positions were graced by heads of religious institutions (*maṭhāpati*) and conducted as a one-way activity.

Bāsavannā also wanted to do away with the priestly class. He told that in his religion, everyone should follow a vocation and earn his living and not to live on charity and alms. With this he also wanted to do away with the Hindu noble act of gift-giving (*dāna*); which according to him encouraged idling and exploitation of the ignorance of the masses. Furthermore, he wanted to see that everyone has a right to worship God personally and not through a priest. His argument was that if someone is hungry he should satisfy it himself, and not through a middleman. To facilitate the devotees in fulfilling this need and since all were not allowed into the temple to worship the idol there, Bāsavannā introduced the concept of *Iṣṭaliṅga*, personal emblem of Śiva, which is different from the static form of *Śivalinga* worshipped in Hindu Śaiva temples. This *Iṣṭaliṅga* is always worn on the person and regularly worshipped. With this he wanted to prevent the devotees from going to temples where the static form of *Śivaliṅga* is worshipped and the priestly classes were patronized, establish themselves as the agents of god. He also wanted to remove the importance given to ritual purity and pollution rules, advocating that by wearing the *Iṣṭaliṅga* always on one's person the physical body, which comes in continuous contact with god, purifies not only the body but also the mind. In this sense, according to Śaraṇas, the human body becomes the abode of Śiva — temple and heaven (*kāyave kailāsa*). This has been illustrated in many of the *vacana*s.

His teachings were meant to liberate the devotees from the clutches of temples and priests. These ideas were novel and dynamic and the whole society was charged with action for change; away from Brāhmaṇical religious order. These discussions later transformed into action and the Śaraṇas including Bāsavannā who was a brāhmaṇa by birth and a minister, started mingling and inter-dining even with untouchables and also stopped going to temples and inviting brāhmaṇa priests to their rituals. This angered the Brāhmaṇical groups and they complained to the king about these unreligious activities. But Bāsavannā convinced the king that the laws of Manu do not apply to the Liṅgāyats who are outside the purview of Hinduism.

Kalyāṇa Krānti

Around 1150 AD the king Bijjala seized Kalyāṇa, the capital of Cāḷukya kingdom. The Cāḷukyas were his relatives but still he ill-treated them and their supporters, and this had earned him a lot of ill-will (Chidanandamurthy, 2001). When Bijjala shifted his capital to Kalyāṇa, and automatically Bāsavannā, the Śaraṇa Liṅgāyats and the religious parliament, followed him. The Vaiṣṇavites who were influential during the Cāḷukya rule in the state administration became less important. Bāsavannā's new religious ideals added some more fuel and the orthodox-minded among both the Śaiva and Vaiṣṇava sects became unhappy. King Bijjala had several queens and one of them came from the Hoysala dynasty, who were Vaiṣṇavites. This queen and her prince had an eye on the position of the successor (*yuvarāja*) although there were other princes too from other queens in the race (Karnad, 1996).

The Brāhmaṇical group in general, and Vaiṣṇavites in particular, who were dissatisfied with the king, and Bāsavannā soon got an opportunity to strike them. The daughter of Madhuvayya, a brāhmaṇa, and the son of Haralayya, an untouchable, after embracing Liṅgāyat religion, got married according to the Śaraṇa tradition and in the presence of Bāsavannā. Since this marriage was against the Hindu *varṇa dharma*, the orthodox-minded brought the matter to the notice of King Bijjala, the protector of the law of the land. When the king in turn asked Bāsavannā for an explanation, the latter justified the marriage quoting that the *varṇa* code of conduct does not apply to the Liṅgāyats. This enraged the Brāhmaṇical group. Keeping the prince in the lead they rebelled against the king, dethroned and imprisoned him and also crowned the prince. Later through him, the married couple's parents were severely punished. Their eyes were taken away and were also imprisoned.

Bāsavannā was shocked at the ghastly turn of the situation. A section of Liṅgāyats who were enraged by now, attacked the new king and also succeeded in dethroning and ousting him out of Kalyāṇa. They once again installed Bijjala on the throne. This was interpreted by their opponents that the Śaraṇa Liṅgāyats have political interests, more than the religious. Later they also mobilized a much bigger force under the same prince and killed a large number of Liṅgāyats/ Śaraṇas, brought down the hall of religious parliament and also set fire to *vacana* volumes stored there. In the mele, a few Śaraṇas, including Bāsavannā, his nephew Channabāsavannā, Allamā, Sidrama and others managed to collect a few volumes of *vacana*s and safely escaped out of Kalyāṇa. They were chased for a long time and for a long distance, till they crossed the state boundaries and it is said that they had gone to unknown destinations. The new protest-religious tradition with its lot of fresh and noble ideals had thus ended in the land of its origin.

Post-Bāsavannā Period

There are no authentic documents to tell as to what happened after the blood revolution and also about the Śaraṇas, who survived, where they went, who were together and what more work they accomplished afterwards and so on. After about two centuries, during the fourteenth century, they emerged under the leadership of four Śaraṇas in different parts of Kannaḍa land, as Śaraṇa Liṅgāyat *dharma*; a populistic religion and society (cf. Ishwaran, 1997).

After the Kalyāṇa Krānti — this is how the suppression of the protest movement of Kalyāṇa came to be known — the Liṅgāyat movement no doubt lost its leaders and the centre of learning and above all several volumes of *vacana* literature was totally destroyed. Those who survived the onslaught, did not surface because of the fear from the Brāhmaṇical group. During the remaining part of the twelfth and the thirteenth centuries, south India especially experienced a lot of political and social turmoil. The kings and their sectarian supporters were always at war with each other and the three Hindu empires of South — the Cāḷukyas, the Rāṣṭrakūṭas and the Hoyasalas, got disintegrated one by one. There was total chaos, lawlessness and uncertainty. This weakness made way for external invasion by the Persians, Turks and the Afghans. The invasion, which was confined to north India, for the first time during the thirteenth century, crossed the Vindhyas. Once again, there was a large scale killing, destruction and looting of wealth from not only the common people but also from the religious institutions and palaces. This continued till the establishment of the Mogul rule over north India, through which most of the invaders came to India.[5]

→ 5. During this period of disturbance, when there were no kings or religious leaders to provide physical and emotional security to the masses, the Sūfī saints took the burden on them. By taking over the dilapidated temples and *maṭhas* they helped the common people by taking them under their wings, comforted and helped them. Since folk Islam and folk Hinduism have many things in common, such as saints and holy men, material offerings to tombs, pilgrimages, self-suffering by inflicting pain on the body, emotion charged dances and singing of devotional songs, resurrection of the dead saint or martyrdom and so on. Sufism, its saints and institutions (*daragāh*) were readily accepted by the masses. (Cf. Saheeb 1997).

When Sūfīs were busy with this smoothening work, the Brāhmaṇical groups had quietly withdrawn to safer position and places. A few literate ones had aligned themselves with the Muslim rulers in their state-administration. This had earned immunity for them and their religious institutions. But majority of low caste Hindu masses who had lost their institutional support were →

During the thirteenth and fourteenth centuries, the Brāhmaṇical groups who were in defensive were now off the back of their opponents including the Liṅgāyats. They were also feeling guilty in a way, for playing their sectarian religious card too far. With the result, the Śaraṇas began to emerge with their religious institutions and *vacana* literature, which had almost gathered dust and was hidden in homes, *maṭhas* and temples. By now, Harihara (1200 AD) a junior contemporary of Bāsavannā, Somanātha (1200 AD), Bhīmakavi (1369 AD) who translated the Somanātha's work, Chāmarasa (1430 AD), Lakkanna Dandeśa (1450 AD), Siṅgirāja (1500) and Ṣaḍākṣarī (1677 AD) and others, from the twelfth to seventeenth century, wrote many epics to elevate Bāsavannā to the level of a hero of Sanskrit epics. A section of Liṅgāyats also made use of these works to elevate Liṅgāyatism to the status of Vedic *dharma* (for more details see Ishwaran 1982: 22-37) and organized the Vīraśaiva *dharma* on the model of a Hindu religion and society with Jaṅgama as the centre.

Sūfīs who had gained foothold by now in south India, found many things in common with Liṅgāyat *dharma* such as opposition to idol-worship, construction of temples, rituals, purity and pollution rules, importance given to birth order and their occupation tolerated the latter and their religious tradition.

Today there are about 70 lakh of Liṅgāyats spread out in the southern states of Karnataka, Maharashtra, Andhra Pradesh and Tamil Nadu. Among these around 60 lakh are in Karnataka (Havanur, 1984). These are only the estimated figures of Liṅgāyats provided by such organizations as Vīraśaiva Mahạsabhā since the caste-wise enumeration of Indian population was stopped from 1971 Indian Census onwards. These figures vary from 70 lakh to 1 crore or even

→ forced to take shelter under Sufism (Islamization of these Indian Muslims came much later during the Mogul ruler Aurangazeb) and in a way that is still going on; the way Sanskritization and Christianization are taking place.

more. The name "Liṅgāyat" has many synonyms such as Vīraśaiva, Vīraśaiva Liṅgāyat, Śaraṇa, Śaraṇa Liṅgāyat Basavaits and so on. It is still debated whether they are a sect among Hindus or a separate religious group (cf. MaCarmic 1963; Parvathamma, 1967; Ishwaran, 1983, 1992; Māte Mahādevī, 1996; Chidanandamurthy, 2001). Those who treat them as Hindus argue that they are a caste and the different occupational groups among them which number 21, are sub-castes of Vīraśaiva Liṅgāyats. Others who have treated them as a sect argue that the occupational groups are castes and not sub-castes. Māte Mahādevī and Ishwaran have treated Liṅgāyats as a separate religious group. To support their arguments they say that the Liṅgāyats do not accept the trinity of god, existence of soul, rebirth, Vedas, *varṇa dharma*, Brāhmaṇical priests, purity and prohibition rules and the existence of different worlds. They instead follow the teachings of Bāsavannā and other Śaraṇas and are guided by the three cardinal principles — *guru, liṅga* and *jaṅgama*, five noble paths of life — *pañcācāra* (*liṅgācāra, sadācāra, śivācāra, gaṇācāra* and *bhṛtyācāra*), six steps *(ṣaṭśālā)* in the path to attain Śiva state (*bhakta, maheśvara, prasāda, prāṇaliṅga, varṇa* and *aikya*) and *aṣṭāvarṇa* principles (*guru, liṅga, jaṅgama, pādodaka, prasada, vibhūti, rudrākṣī* and *mantra*). Some of these concepts sound Hinduized in their nomenclatures since Śaraṇa *dharma* is a protest-religion of Hinduism. But their meaning, ideology and interpretation are totally different from the Brāhmaṇical ideals. Here importance is given to life on the earth. *Liṅga* means the *Iṣṭaliṅga*, Jaṅgama means not the Vīraśaiva priest but change of state and society (Ishwaran, 1982). They also do not recognize any type of discrimination and claim that theirs is a casteless and classless society.

Whether the Liṅgāyat are Hindus or a sect or a separate religious group is a moot point. After the Kalyāṇa Krānti, Sanskritization had set into the Śaraṇa ideals. Added to that was the fact that all Liṅgāyats were, Śaivaites and all of them wore the emblem of Śiva on their person and worship it individually. Further their rites and rituals are family-centred and are performed by the householder himself under the supervision of a Jangama and not a brāhmaṇa priest. Performance of mass scale rituals is also opposed and so very little importance or roles are given to the Jaṅgama priest. Ideally, there is no priestly class (caste) among the Liṅgāyats. When an occasion arises, the householder performs the rituals and an elderly and experienced person supervises it.

As a protest religion, the Liṅgāyatism pose certain problems for study. For any religious tradition to function and survive as a separate tradition, it requires four components — a holy book, religious institutions, priests (ritual performances) and devotees. As has already been noted it is a protest-religion, the Liṅgāyatism never advocated any of them. The only source of study left is through the devotees and their religious life. But even this is not of much help since a section of them have Sanskritized their way of life and became known as Vīraśaiva Liṅgāyats.[6]

Secondly, the Śaraṇa Liṅgāyat had also discarded all types of religious institutions — *maṭha*s and temples — and so there are no religious leaders — priests. With the exodus of Śaraṇas from Kalyāṇa and pulling down of *anubhava maṇḍapa*, they had also lost their guidance and leadership from Kalyāṇa. Those

6. The Vīraśaiva Liṅgāyats have their own priestly group — Jaṅgama, who claim the top place in hierarchy. These Jaṅgamas, in their race to establish an equal status with the brāhmaṇa priests, claim their origin to the five-faced (*pañcamukha*) Śiva, and from each one emerged a divine teacher (*ārādhya guru*), who together established five holy seats (*pīṭha*). Often calling themselves Liṅgī brāhmaṇas, these Jaṅgamas have learnt Sanskrit and studied Vedas, Āgamas and Purāṇas. They observe an elaborate rite to initiate novices to Jaṅgamahood (*iyyācāra dīkṣa*). Among themselves these *maṭha*s have divided the Vīraśaiva devotees and attend to their day-to-day religious ritual needs. Each *maṭha* has its branches and agents who are Vīraśaiva Jaṅgamas by birth and householders, in all major towns and villages, where their linked-devotees reside. They function like the brāhmaṇa priests and expect that all rites, rituals and celebrations be conducted with their approval. Any violation is punished by a ritual boycott. (For details see Nadhimath, 1979; Ishwaran, 1997.)

few Śaraṇas who had stayed behind in Kalyāṇa after the revolution, had abandoned or altered their Śaraṇa ideals and came under the influence of Sanskritic ritual tradition. Later, they became known as Hindu Vīraśaivas or Vīraśaiva Liṅgāyats, meaning, the Śivas who possess the knowledge of Vedas, and finally became a caste under Hinduism. The Liṅgāyat (Liṅga + Āyat) means those who received, wear and worship Śiva in the emblem form, moulded in a mixture of waterproof black wax and other ingredients — *kante*. This is again a figure of speech and here it means holy dress, garb, cover or smear. The Vīraśaiva Liṅgāyats who differentiated themselves from the Śaraṇas, got the *liṅgam* moulded out of this wax and placing within it a mini form of the *Sthāvaraliṅga*, the emblem of Śiva worshipped in the Hindu Śaiva temples.[7] But those who were away from the epicentre of this counter-revolution, continued to lead the life of Śaraṇas and they are the focus of this study.

---

7. The *sthāvara* (static, stationary, fixed, crystallized) *liṅgam* itself is the result of the union of *bṛhat yoni* (Great clitoris symbolizing mother goddess) with the male element (*puruṣa-Śiva*) which is planted in the upright position. This is the reminiscence of the phallic worship tradition and in similar to the Greek symbol Omega (Ω), but in a horizontal position. (Cf. Chidanandamurthy, 1964, Gurumurthy, 1996, 1997.)

   According to Hindu belief, it is only the gods who with their consorts become active and fruitful. To symbolize this capacity, they are always named, visualized, sculptured and pictured together (Śiva-Pārvatī, Sītā-Rāma, Girijā-Śaṅkara, Lakṣmī-Ramaṇa and so on). With this belief and form, the male and female elements are carved and put together in the activated *liṅgam* form. Therefore this is moulded in black wax (*kante* — here black colour symbolizes not only the darkness in the *sanctum sanctorum* to create privacy for the gods, but also the ignorance in the devotees) and in oval (shape of the tower over the *sanctum sanctorum* of a temple) shape. Though the Vīraśaiva Liṅgāyats wear this emblem on their person around their neck, placing it in a silver casket (*karadige*), suspended by a string of sacred thread (*Śivadara*), they visualize that they are carrying or wearing a Śiva temple with them.

The *liṅgam* worn and worshipped by Śaraṇas is known as *Iṣṭaliṅga* and moulded without the mini model of *Sthāvaraliṅga*. The Śaraṇa vision and view of the *liṅga* is the flame on the lit lamp wick; meaning the knowledge, great awareness (*ariwu*) about oneself (know thyself), to indicate that they are enlightened persons. This awareness is about the questions, who they are, how they are different from the Hindus, why they do not follow the Vedic religious tradition and so on. This knowledge that there is nothing inside the *Iṣṭaliṅga* (*śūnya sampādana jñāna*), is a basic requirement of a Śaraṇa (cf. Mahadevaiah and Tipperudraswamy, 1963). This kind of spiritual knowledge is given to the novice before they are initiated to Śaraṇahood and knowledge is most essential for a Śaraṇa Liṅgāyat as there are no religious institutions, sacred books and specialists to guide him in life; which in fact are found in other religious traditions including the Hinduism.[8]

"Death" in Liṅgāyatism

Here, we have taken a set of ceremonies and celebrations, observed by the Liṅgāyats Śaraṇas to mark the changes in the status of an individual, as source material to understand their religious tradition (Gurumurthy, 1997, 2002). Among these we are concerned here with death. The Liṅgāyats believe in "death." They believe that there is something similar to the soul in man, which is known as "Great Openness" (*mahābayalu*). To denote these Liṅgāyats the terms "Openness" and "Great Openness" (*bayalu* and *mahābayalu* or *nibbayalu*) have been used. They do not believe in rebirth, transmigration

8. The Liṅgāyat Śaraṇa does not observe rites and rituals the way the Brāhmaṇical groups do. Instead they have ceremonies and celebrations to get social and economic approval (not rituals). In the strict Vedic sense, these rites and rituals are prescribed and on attainment of certain stage in life, an individual must undergo these rituals. But according to Śaraṇa Liṅgāyats, these occur normally in an individual on attaining certain age. So observing and explaining them with a religious ritual is not acceptable to them. Instead, they observe the life-crisis occasions as celebrations and without the official priest.

of soul and existence of different worlds. Birth means occupation of some part of this openness (space) by erecting (body) walls. This means the space within the walls and outside walls is the same. Death means flattening of these walls and merging of the space between the walls with the space outside. In this sense Śaraṇas have termed death as *bayalāguvudu* which means "to become one" with "Great Openness" — the god (*nibbayalāguvudu*). With death, the walls are flattened and nothing happens to the space.

This explanation is similar to the Hindu Monism Philosophy (Advaita). This is well illustrated in the *vacana*s of Śaraṇas. But what is different and unique with Śaraṇa Liṅgāyat philosophy is that, at no point of time the individual is viewed as detached or separated from god. Contrary to this, in Hindu theology, some part of god (*ātmā* — soul) separates from Him (*paramātmā*), just as water separates from sea through evaporation and goes up in the sky to cool and comes down to earth in the form of rain, to merge into the same sea, through many religious streams. In the meantime, the water collects the colour and taste of the soil through which it flows, a soul also collects merits and demerits, by doing good and bad things in each birth. On the basis of the report given on these deeds by the attendants of god of death (Yama *dharma*), the soul is sent to hell or heaven to harvest benefits.

At this stage, two questions arise about the Hindu view of good or bad deeds. One, why god who is omniscient and omnipresent allows man to do bad deeds. Two, why and how man forgets the harsh punishments that he gets while in hell and repeat the same bad deeds during his next births. To answer these questions the Hindu tradition has taken shelter under the illusionary concept of *karma* and the river of "Forgetfulness" which flows between the worlds of Hell and Earth.

But the Śaraṇas have successfully and very clearly explained these questions by comparing births and deaths with the concepts of "oneness." According to this explanation, a man is always good since he is always found united with the god. To exhibit this, they always wear the *Iṣṭaliṅga* on their person. With this notion they worship their own body (*kāya*), with the sacred ash and leaves, which are used in worshipping the god. This is not just a belief but is also practised in daily life. For example, when two Śaraṇas meet, they greet each other as if they are paying obeisance to god — Śiva and by enquiring "Whether worship of oneself is over"or "whether offering of sacred food to oneself is over," to enquire whether they have performed the Śiva worship and eaten food. This shows that they never view the worship or feeding is made to someone outside oneself or to someone other than themselves.

The state of death is also viewed differently by the Śaraṇa Liṅgāyats. According to them, there is either birth or rebirth. The state of birth and death that the other religions view, are like waves formed and merged on a high sea. This means man (soul) never gets separated from god. So no separation and incorporation rites are performed to individual on "death." In fact, the observances arranged to mark "death" are termed as "assemblies" of fellow believers (Śaraṇa Sammelana). They assemble to remember and spread the good qualities the person had in him so that others can emulate them. Like this "death" is celebrated by the Śaraṇa Liṅgāyats (*Maranave Mahānavamī*). Except these no rites of (permanent) separation and reunification as shown by Von Gannep (1960) are performed. This has been clearly expressed in the *vacana*s of "Śaraṇas."[9]

9. This lack of ritual value to death brought changes in the social and economic aspects of the society. As has been noted earlier, Bāsavannā founded the new religion to do away with all kinds of discriminations in all aspects of life. This attracted the common people belonging to different religions, castes and creeds towards Liṅgāyatism. As a result occupational idenitities were lost and these came to be known as vocations (*kāyaka*) and anybody who liked or had proficiency in a vocation could follow that vocation. With the elimination of traditional support to the occupations, different occupational groups came together as guilds →

The activities conducted by the Śaraṇa at the time of "death" are as follows: Soon as the news of death in any family of their guild is learnt, they visit the family as a social obligation, to share their grief, monetary and physical burden involved in performing the funeral activities. Since death does not bring ritual prohibition, the members of the mourning family according to their convenience, fix the day, time and place of the funeral and send words to their kith and kin residing within and outside the village. Secondly, they also formally send words to all the members of their occupational guild to come and help them in disposing of the corpse. On arrival, they undertake different activities, according to their vocation, such as conveying the news of death, digging the burial pit, construction of a bamboo bier, providing pipe music for the funeral procession and procuring of the funerary assemblage needed.

The kith and kin come to the mourning family with sacred leaves, cakes of sacred ash and incense sticks, which are needed in performing worship. After showering a few sacred leaves on the corpse, the rest of the leaves are kept by the side of the "dead." Since the Śaraṇa Liṅgāyats do not recognize death pollution, the visitors are free to visit the homes of other Liṅgāyats in the community and also accept hospitality of food

---

→ (*āyadagumpu* or *āyadakūta*) (Ishwaran, 1966; Gurumurthy, 1976). In this social set-up, unlike in the Hindu Jaimanī system (Wisor 1938; Oscar Lewis, 1958), interpersonal relations became reciprocal rather than binding in the name of religion. Moral rather than religious obligations constituted as the means to control the occupational groups in a community. When a life-crisis occurs in a family of a Liṅgāyat, other members readily extended their help. There were no masters and servants, high and low among the occupational groups. The Śaraṇa made this possible since the life crises are not associated with rites and rituals. These are observed or celebrated only to mark and publicize the change that occurs in the status (socio-religious), roles and residence of the individuals. When other traditions introduced ritual approval, the Śaraṇas introduced moral and societal approval to mark these stages.

or drink from them. When all the expected kith and kin and members of the guild have assembled and the arrangements for the burial are made, the corpse accompanied by the entire gathering of mourners, i.e., men, women, children and the preceptor of the dead is taken to the burial ground[10] and it is buried in a pit, in a sitting posture. The *Iṣṭaliṅga* of the person

10. At the entrance to funeral ground (*rudrabhūmi*), the Vīraśaivas enact a scene wherein a few persons from the procession walk little ahead and stand there posing as *śivagaṇa*s in charge of the entrance to Kailāsa. As the procession approaches, they stop them with the warning words, as to who they are and why they are entering the Kailāsa. For this, one of them who leads the procession, identifies the dead to them and tells that this Śivagaṅgā intends to come back to Kailāsa. In reply to this, they demand what merits he had earned to come there. For this, they narrate the meritorious deeds done by him in life such as gifting of food, clothing, cattle, land and cash; which are considered meritorious acts in Vedic religion and requests for permission to admit him into heaven. Convinced of his merits, the *śivagaṇa*s ask them to wait there itself till they get the approval of Kailāsapati-Śiva. Then they walk up to the burial pit and return to the entrance with a few sacred leaves and cakes of sacred ash and tell that the permission is granted. They also convey that Śiva is anxious to meet and listen about the meritorious deeds, accomplished by the Vīraśaiva. As an invitation to him from Śiva, they hand over the sacred objects they had brought with them. They also tell that since all cannot enter Kailāsa, until their time has come and they have earned merit in life, they ask those who have brought the body to hand the same over to them so that they can take it to heaven. To symbolize this, from there they carry the bier. However, others also follow them to the burial pit (*samādhi-sthala*).

For the Vīraśaiva Liṅgāyat, the burial location and design of the pit and its arrangements are all ritually important since it is going to house the body of a *śivagaṇa* who is going to attain the state of meditation, *samādhi* (this is a Sūfī tradition, as the Sūfīs construct a tomb for their peer who is going to live thereafter his resurrection). Therefore, the family priest of a Vīraśaiva Liṅgāyat selects a suitable spot, sanctifies it and also gives the required specification to dig the pit, so that it would be suitable for meditation.

→

is placed in his/her right palm as if he is sitting for Śiva worship. So the funerary furniture includes sacred ash, water, leaves, lit oil lamp and incense sticks.[11] While the arrangements are being made for burial the Śaraṇas assemble to say a few words in memory of the departed member. Finally as a mark of bidding farewell, they shower sacred leaves into the burial pit. Later the pit is covered with the same excavated soil. Since "death" means becoming one with "Openness," this is the last formal activity of a funeral. No tomb structure is constructed

---

→ Since Viraśaiva Liṅgāyat are Sanskritized and believe in death, on arrival at the funeral ground, the corpse is placed on one pit and the spouse of the person is made to sit by the side to perform the separation rite for the couple and widowhood rite to the surviving spouse. If the widowed is a woman, the five *maṅgala* objects, which are worn by married women, are removed and placed on the lap of her husband. This means with him goes her status; in other words she too is going with him. Death also brings ritual pollution to the Vīraśaiva. So, all the participants as a must go to a water source and take a ritual bath to come out of the pollution state. The primary mourners, however, continue to be in that state till it is formally removed by observing a minor rite. Here the Vīraśaiva Jaṅgama priests, who claim to be outside the ritual pollution sphere, help them by performing a ritual (for detailed description of Vīraśaiva rites see Gubbannavar, 1984; Salimath, 1959; Hiremath 1961).

11. Over the years, because of Sanskritization, like other passage rites, the Vīraśaiva have started observing elaborate funeral rites and also construct tomb structures. When this was condemned by the Śaraṇa Liṅgāyat and the Brāhmaṇical groups that as "śūdra" they have no passage rites including the funeral rite, they have started even glorifying death by observing many more rituals. Jaṅgama priest who is supposed to be in charge of the funeral activities is brought in a ceremonial way. Taking charge of the dying person, he performs *vibhūtivilaya*, a minor rite, in which the person is taken to a state similar to *vānaprasthāśrama* of Hindus. For this, the person is symbolically bathed and his entire body is smeared with sacred ash. His personal emblem of Śiva is taken out of the silver casket and tied to his right palm with a piece of new cloth, as if he is in the process of entering into or becoming one with the *liṅgam* (*liṅgaikya*).

for a Śaraṇa Liṅgāyat.[12]

---

12. To this now the element of resurrection is added which might have come from Sufism and according to their view death is temporary wherein the person is believed to have gone to the heavens, i.e., he is in meditation (*samādhi*), to hold communion with divine forces or even god. The time taken for the communion varies according to the religious tradition. When the communion is over, the individual is believed to have returned to earth with more power and wisdom to serve the humanity. Hence, this occasion is observed as the day of resurrection and devotees throng the sacred centre to receive some part of this merit for themselves. Often, depending upon the religious tradition, the merit is distributed through sacred food or gospel to the assembly. The Vīraśaiva Liṅgāyats celebrate the occasion as *śānti samārambha* or *śiva gaṇārādhane*. Because of the Sanskritization, they believe that an individual — *śivagaṇa*, comes to earth on some specific assignment (*nimitta*) from Lord Śiva and shuttles between two worlds to report on the progress made and to seek further guidance in his assignment. The day of his returning is seen as resurrection and his tomb becomes an active pilgrimage centre and the day becomes a grand festival occasion and a source of income to the priestly group.

    When a *śivagaṇa* returns he is believed to have brought a fund of spiritual knowledge or power and distributes it to a congregation. A pot (*gaṭa*) with brim full of water is established (*sthāpanā*) to signify the fund of wisdom brought by him from the heaven. This is placed in a prominent place and worshipped. The god's representative on earth the Jaṅgama and a few others address the gathering on spiritual matters. This is interpreted that the resurrected person is speaking through them. The congregation is followed by mass feeding of sacred festive foods (*prasāda*).

    The Vīraśaiva, when constructing a tomb for the dead also makes provision for a niche in the wall facing north, the auspicious direction for the Hindus. This niche is later used for keeping a sacred lamp. This symbolically means construction of Śiva temple over the grave pit of a *śivagaṇa*, who has become Śiva (*śivaikya*). To prepare ritual ground for this the grave pit dug by the untouchables is later sanctified by sprinkling water in which the holy feet of Jaṅgama priest are washed (*pādodaka*). By the time the pit is ready, the corpse is washed and dressed in a sack like one-piece dress, usually worn by the Hindu ascetics. This symbolizes that the person has now entered the fourth "stage in

→

Śaraṇa Liṅgāyats also do not believe in eternal bondage between the married couple. Married couple for them means life companions (*jīvana saṅgati*) who came together in an understanding and through individual and familial contact and not by chance or because of matching of horoscopes. They come together to lead a morally, socially and religiously good life, which is expected of the Śaraṇas. The husband or wife does not get any special right, duty or obligation on each other and certainly not the way a Hindu husband *patiparameśvara* gets. The couple view and treat each other with mutual respect and equality first as a Śaraṇa Liṅgāyat and then a fellow traveller and companion, in the journey towards each other's well-being (*kalyāṇa*), a life which is expected of a Liṅgāyat. In this sense, the Śaraṇa Liṅgāyats have used the word *Kalyāṇa Mahotsava* for marriage (not *vivāh, kanyādāna*).

When one of them stops (because of death) or discontinues (because of divorce or desertion) the journey, the other, after completing the expected observances, teams up with someone else found suitable and continues the journey towards *kalyāṇa* — the state of attainment of Śivahood. With this view the Śaraṇa Liṅgāyats allow remarriage (widow and widower) and such couple do not have any stigma in society. "Widows" do not attract any type of inauspiciousness nor alter their dress or hairstyle, food and living habits. They continue to hold familial and personal properties, adopt children and also attend observances and celebrations performed in the community. They can also extend invitations in their name, for the marriage of their children and such other happy celebrations. They continue to wear the *Iṣṭaliṅga* on their person and also

→ life" — *saṁnyāsa āśrama*. Earlier to that, his family gifts away foodgrains, pieces of new cloth, etc., to *jamānī* servants, needy poor and cattle and landed property is given to priests, *maṭha*s and temples. This indicates two things: one that he is leaving the earthly world for good or in other words, that the Vīraśaiva believes in death. Secondly, by giving away the material wealth he overcomes worldly desires (*māyā*) and also collects enough merit in life to get him a place in the heavens.

personally worship it. In fact, for Liṅgāyat women, the sacred ash (*bhabhūti*) and the *Iṣṭaliṅga* are important and not the five sacred objects (*maṅgalasūtra*, glass bangles, toe and nose rings and vermilion, *sindūra*, on the forehead) prescribed for Hindu married women. Thus, they continue to wear them even after parting from their husband.

References

Bhima Kavi, 1971, *Basava Purāṇa*, Dharwad: Karnatak University, Kannaḍa.

Chamanasa, 1430 AD, *Prabhulingaleela*, Leaf manuscript, Kannaḍa.

Chidanandamurthy, M., 1966, *Śāsanagala Sānskṛtika Adhyayana*, Mysore: Mysore University, Kannaḍa.

———, 2000, *Vīraśaiva Dharma: Bhāratīya Sanskriti* (*Hindu: Lingāyata*) (Kannaḍa), Bangalore: Minchu Prakshana.

Gubbannavar, Śivananda, 1984, *Lingāyata Sanskāragalu*, Dharwad: Prasaranga, Karnatak University, Kannaḍa.

Gurumurthy, K.G., *Kallapura*: *A South Indian Village*, Dharwad: Karanatak University Press.

———, 1997, *Passage Rites in a Protest Religious Tradition*, M.S. Three Lectures delivered under L.K. Anantha Krishna Iyer Endowment Lecture Series, University of Madras, Madras.

———, 1996, *Dharma Mattu Rājakīya: A Cultural Study of the Sacred Complex of Sri Renuka Yallamma Punya Kshetra Athani*, Vimochana Prakashana, Kannaḍa.

———, 1996, *Isthalinga: "Kalpane Hagu Bhāvane,"* Taralabalu Hunnime Commemorative Volume Ranebennur, Celebration Committee.

———, 2002, *Lingāyata Dhārmika Sampradāya mattu Sānskṛtikaraṇa*, Kannaḍa, In Press.

Harihara Kavi, 1938, *Basavarajadevara Ragale*, Mysore: Wesley Press and Publication House.

Havanur, L.G., 1984, Report of the 2nd Backward Class and Castes Commission, Submitted to Government of Karanataka, Banagalore.

Hiremath, Basavaiah Shastri, 1961, *Antyasaṁskāra Vidhāna*, Gadag, Sri Śivananda Book Depot, Kannaḍa.

Ishwaran, K., 1966, *Tradition and Economy in Village India*, Bombay, Asia.

———, 1977, *A Populistic Community and Modernization in India, Leiden*, E.J. Brill.

———, 1982, *Religion and Society among the Lingāyats of South India*, New Delhi, Vikas.

———, 1992, *Speaking of Basava: Lingāyat Religion and Culture in South Asia*, Oxford, West View Press.

———, 1997, *Lingāyata, Jaina Mattu Brahmana Dharmagala Mathagala ondu Tulanathmika Adhyayana*, Bangalore, Priyadharshini Prakashana, (Kannaḍa).

Karnad Girish, 1990, *Tale Danda*, Dharwad, Manohara Grantah Bhandhara (Kannaḍa Drama on the last days of Bāsavannā and Bijjala in Kalyāṇa.

Lakkanna Dandesa, 1960, *Śiva Tattva Cintamani*, Mysore, University of Mysore (a fifteenth century manuscripts).

Mātaji (Māte Mahādevi), 1996, *Lignāyatharu Viraśivaralla* (*Śpastha Vivarane*) (*Lingāyatas are not Vīraśaivas — a clarification*), Bangalore, Vishwakalyana Mission.

MaCormick, W., 1963, "Lingāyathas as a Sect," *Journal of Royal Anthropological Institute*, 93:1:59-71.

Menezes, L.M.A. and Angadi S.M. 1967, *Vavanas of Basavanna*, With an introduction by H.H. Taralabalu Jagadguru Sri Śri Śivācārya Sirigere, Annana Balaga. (A Translation of 327 out of 955 *Vacanas* of Bāsavannā to English.)

Nandhimath, S.C., 1979, *Handbook of Vīrashaivism*, New Delhi, Motilal Banarasidass (Originally published in 1942).

Narayana, P.V., 1997, *Vachana Sahitya*, Banglore, Sharana Sampada, Akhila Bharatha Sharana Sahitya Parishat, (Kannaḍa).

Oscar Lawis, 1958, *Village Life in Northern India: Studies in a Delhi Village*, Illinois, University of Illinois Press.

Parvathamma, C., 1967, "The Social Structure of Lingāyats: A Sectarian caste of Mysore," *Journal of Sociology and Applied Research*, Jabalpur University, 1967:1:1.

Sadaksari, 1968, *Basavaraja Vijayam*, Dharwad, Karnatak University, (fourteenth century Kannaḍa script).

Salimath, Channaveera, 1959, *Vīraśaiva Daśarūpa Athavā Purohita Kaipidi*, Gadag, P.C. Shabadimath (Kannaḍa).

Saheeb, A.A.S., 1998, *Nagore-E-Sharief: A Sacred Complex Study*, Ph.D. thesis accepted by Karnatak University for a doctorate degree in Anthropology.

Singiraja Kavi, 1970, *Basavarāja Carita*, Mysore, University of Mysore.

Sivagana Prasādi Mahādēvaiah, *Śūnya Sampādane*, vol. I, Chitradurga, Sri Brihanmath Samsthana.

Srinivas, M.N., 1952, *Religion and Society among the Coorgs of South India*, Oxford, Clarendon Press.

———, 1956, "A Note on Sankritization and Westernization," *Far Eastern Quarterly*, XV, no. 4, 1956, pp. 481-96.

Tipperudraswamy, H., 1963, *Śūnya Sampādane*, Mysore, D.V.K. Murthy, Kannaḍa.

Von Gannep, Arnald, 1960, *Rites of Passage*, Chicago: The University of Chicago Press.

Wisor, W.H., 1938, *Hindu Jajmani System: Socio-economic systems interrelating members of a Hindu village community in services*, Lucknow: Lucknow Publishing House (Reprinted in 1958).

5

Death

End of Life or Beginning of a New One?

Majeed Khan
Connie Kitchens
R. Paul Firnhaber

EVERY human being experiences death in the form of sleep, coma, faint and trance in his lifetime. When he gets up or come out of faintness or coma, he does not know what happened to him while he was sleeping or was under the influence of faint. Death occurs at several levels. Scientifically speaking, somatic death is the death of the organism as a whole; it is marked by cessation of heartbeat, respiration, movement and brain activity. Clotting of the blood begins shortly after death and the decomposition which follows is caused by the action of enzymes and bacteria. Although brain cells may survive for not more than five minutes after somatic death, those of the heart can survive for about 15 minutes and those of the kidney for about 30 minutes. That is why, immediately after a person's death, the organs of his body can be transplanted into a living person.

However, in the modern medical science the concept of brain-death is accepted as the human death. A majority of the states in the United States and in several countries of Europe had accepted brain-death as an essential sign of death by the late 1980s. According to this view the sign of death is the absence of activity in the higher centres of the brain principally the neocortex. Thus in a strict medical term, the death results in stopping the function of heart, ceasing breathing and the person's sense of smell, touch, see, hear, feel, taste, think, etc., and making the body absoluntely cold. The body will never be alive again and shall decompose in the process of time.

Whatever is the medical or scientific concept of death, the religious and philosophical concept is quite different. Each religion has its own philosophy and concept of death. Origin of religion and faith in God is totally based on the concept of life after death.

God is a great Creator, who likes variety and colourful beauty on this earth; it is why the geography, topography, climate, animals, plants and trees are all different in different parts of the world. Likewise, the human beings are also different and a variety of colourful human races can be seen in various parts of the world. Similarly, if God also sends religion, we can see the variety of different religious ideas and concepts in various parts of this world. Thus all religions lead us towards one supreme Creator — God — and as such all religions must be true and created by God.

If it is so, all of us should believe in other's religion and consider each religion as a true one, leading towards God, the Supreme Power of the universe; but it is not so, each one of us considers his own religion as the true one and all other religions as false. If we look at the basic concept lying under each religion, we shall find that it deals with social welfare and is in the best interests of the human society. It is, therefore, most likely, that we, the human beings, created the religions. In return to what God has given to us, religion is the best return. But, those generous people who call themselves as the messengers of God and who played an important role in the creation of religions, such as Abraham, Moses, Jesus, Mohammad, Buddha, the Hindu gods such as Kṛṣṇa, Viṣṇu and Rāma, etc., had one thing in their mind, the purity of social life, the reality of life after death and punishment for hidden and unexposed deeds after death. If the concept of life after death is taken out of any religion, it will melt like ice. There would be then no believer, no worshipper, no God and no religion. It is why that in all religions, Hinduism, Islam, Christianity, Buddhism and whatsoever, the concept of life-after-death is adopted.

In the West, on the one hand we have the humanist/ evolutionary biological view where human beings are animals in a biological system without soul or spiritual essence. On the other, we have the dominant religious approach (Islam and Christianity) in which individuals only live once and then go on to some heaven or hell where they stay for eternity. According to some other school of thought, lives which are lived wrongly, result in painful after lives, and painful subsequent incarnation (Buddhism and Hinduism). Thus Islam and Christianity speak of an eternal afterlife while Buddhism and Hinduism both believe in reincarnation.

In all religions the concept of continuity of life-after-death does exist in one form or other. This continuity is the basic element of all religions and is accepted by all believers. Two examples may be used:

> I personally find it impossible to regard Handel's "Largeo", Keat's "Ode to a Grecian Urn" and the higher ethics as mere by-products of the chemical interaction of a collection of hydrocarbon molecules. With energy, matter, space and time continuous, with nothing lost or wasted, are we ourselves the only manifestation that comes to an end, ceases, is annihilated at three scores years and ten?
>
> — *Soul An Archaeology*, ed. Phil Cousineau

What we call the spirit of man makes new compounds, plays with the laws of chemical action, guides the forces of the atom, changes the face of the earth, gives life to new forms and takes it away from millions of animals and plants. Here is a flame that controls its own flaming, a creative spirit which cannot reasonably be less than the continuity it controls, this thing, soul, mind or spirit, cannot well be exception. In some way, as yet impossible to define, it, too, must possess continuity (D. Curtis, American Astrophysicist, 1872-1942).

Now there is a question of justice and injustice to decide evil and good deeds of individuals. We believe that cosmos is ethically in balance and that there is justice. In such case the death of a child by cancer or accident can be justified in the Hindu or Buddha religions by tracing the cause of such events to the actions of these children in their previous lives but how could this be justified in Islam, Judaism or Christianity.

Christianity and Judaism try to deal with injustice by first claiming that God's injustice tests man's faith and second by quoting *Exodus* (20:5) where God says He will "punish the children for the sins of their parents to the third generations." There apparently seems to be no explanation for this injustice punishing the children for the sins of their elders. It is said that the believer should remain faithful to his God, who can test him in such painful and unjust ways. As God is so far above human beings, he can test them as a teacher tests his students, by incurring sickness, violence and unhappiness upon him.

The notion that children should be punished for their ancestor's sins clearly contradicts modern concepts of justice, which are based on the idea of individual responsibility (as opposed to group responsibility in the *Old Testament*).

There is another dualistic system where God opposes the devil and then makes the devil responsible for injustice. This is problematic since it is almost always claimed that God created the devil and the creator or a powerful being who is the source of evil and injustice is at least partly responsible for such evil, even if the devil is acting out of free will. Islam, Christianity and Judaism fail to resolve this problem, which is the basis of the rejection of a religion by many people.

The term Vedic is often used to describe the three faiths that arose historically from within India and which share a common root in Vedic culture. These faiths are Hinduism,

Buddhism and Jainism. One of the fundamental elements in these three religions is the doctrine of reincarnation. Human beings die and are reborn over and over again. Although, the human life-cycle of birth and rebirth in different forms of physical appearances (human or animal) is found in the Buddhism and Hinduism, there is ambiguity about the animal and plant life.

The production or developmenet of *karma*, meaning action or dead, is what binds the soul or sense of self, to this physical world and to the cycle of rebirth and reincarnation. Only when all *karma*s have been removed or balanced out the soul can be freed from rebirth, and be reunited with God.

In other religions such as Sikhism and Taoism, the concept of death and life is somewhat different. For instance, Taoism is unique in world religions in that it teaches that immortality is achieved by preserving the human, mortal body. It is believed that becoming immortal involves changing the body into an imperishable form. The idea is to become one with the Tao, the flow of nature, and thus to ensure that the body never dies.

The Egyptians believed that the mummified body was the home for this soul or spirit. If the body was destroyed, the spirit might be lost. The idea of spirit was complex involving three real spirits: the *ka, ba* and *akh*. The *ka*, "double" of the person, would remain in the tomb and needed the offerings and objects there. The *ba*, or the "soul," was free to fly out of the tomb and return to it. And it was the *akh*, perhaps translated as "spirit," which had to travel through the Underworld to the Final Judgement and entre to the Afterlife. Thus, the soul of the dead people lived among gods but did not completely leave the land of the living.

In Sikhism the belief is that God created everything, so all life is good, but attachment to the material things of life leads to reincarnation and rebirth. After death God judges each soul, and if it is pure enough, it will rest with Him instead of being reborn again.

When Prince Siddhartha Gautama (the Buddha) began his process of awakening, it is said that his first stage of meditation involved remembering his past lives. In Buddhism it is believed that a similar process (the *jivamala*), can be revealed to others who are on the spiritual path. Thus by meditation and extreme spiritual devotion one can see his past lives.

Other religions have different concepts of life and death. The Abrahamic faiths, meaning those faiths that can trace their tradition back to Prophet Abraham, such as Judaism, Christianity and Islam, are all closely connected historically. For instance, the Christianity arise out of Judaism and rapidly became a separate religion. Islam seeing itself as adding on, correcting and completing the Jewish and Christian scriptures, which form the Islamic perspectives are regarded as being incomplete and flawed accounts of God's revelation.

All three of these faiths believe that we have but one earthly life to live and that there is life after death. Although the specific beliefs differ somewhat, both the Christianity and Islam teachings tell us that there will be a Day of Judgement when God will judge the dead and bring the good to Heaven while casting away the evil. In Judaism it is slightly different in that according to some text when Messiah comes all the just will be raised and all the damned will be cast into hell.

This assumes a wide variety of forms in different religions but some such notion is common to nearly all. Afterlife may be conceived as eternal or beyond time, everlasting, without end or even temporary, subject to cessation through release or absorption into a greater reality or into deity. It need not imply survival of the whole embodied person, survival of a disembodied soul being frequently postulated. Shall we believe that the soul, which is invisible and which goes hence to a place that is like herself, glorious and pure and invisible, to have, which is rightly called the unseen world to dwell with the good and wise God (whither, if it be the will of God, my soul too must shortly go) . . . shall we believe that the soul, whose nature is so glorious and pure and invisible, is blown away by the wind and perishes as soon as she leaves the body, as the world says? (Socrates, *The Phaedo*).

An American lady Janicae is a channeller. She channels a group that she calls *The Celestines*. It is a group of 12 spiritual entities. This is not some sort of mysterious, weird kind of seance. Nor it is some sort of game. It has nothing to do with seances and actually it is as simple as just sitting in a lovely quiet room with friends and having conversation with a visitor. In one of the sessions with Connie Kitchens, the co-author, I asked the Celestine group some questions concerning Death.

Connie: I am writing a paper, co-authoring with Majeed Khan. This is on the subject of "death," the philosophy of it. I was wondering if you could give me some insights or direct me to some place to get more information that would be profitable for this! I want to bring to the readers of this paper the insight and understanding about what death is really about and the afterlife.

Answer: There is no death. Therefore you have to state it a little different. You might say — the passing of the physical body, because you are not in that body. It is just a home for you while you are on the physical earth. Example — just like the Turtle shell is the home of the Turtle. Something you are given to help protect the inner life, the inner beauty, which is the essence of you. We believe that your (Connie's) belief of death is "the finalization of the physical body," and that is exactly right. The conclusion of most religions is that there is an afterlife. That is right. The unknown of where you go and what happens to you when you let go of the shell or the home you were living in — that is the question that most people worry about. The only reason that you have been taught is that death is final. This fear of death has been created so that they can control you while you are here in this physical shell of the human flesh. They (those who perpetrate the lie of death being final) create so much fear in you that you are afraid to breath almost, and that way they can control you, and manipulate you like they want to. Those in power, it could be a certain church, it could be a certain person, it can be a certain belief system, which is totally false. They believe, you are not an individual, and (that) you have own connection and you are in direct contact with God.

In one of her letters to me Connie wrote about her profound experience that had cemented her belief in the continuity of life and reincarnation. She writes, "I had a major heart attack in July 1993. I was 42 and lived in Oklahoma City. I was taken to the hospital, emergency room, where at one point I was actually pronounced dead, only to be revived immediately following this occurrence. At this point I was actually out, in a coma for three days. For what I am about to tell you now some may say that I was dreaming, or this was my imagination running wild. Think as you wish, but I know without a shadow of doubt that what I experienced was real, and I indeed had taken a very unique journey. Some people called it a near-death experience. You may refer to it however you wish. Well, what I remember is that I left my body and immediately entered a bright tunnel of light where I met and was escorted to by who I knew to be Jesus. He took me to what I can only describe as a very large, very beautiful and brilliantly lit room filled with beautiful beings whose love I could feel deeply, whereupon, a very ornate throne, sat God. My feeling of God was that of a loving father, someone I was not afraid, He was touchable and someone I could speak to with confidence. He was right there and I knew that no matter where I was He would be there. I could not be without God! I must also say that during all this time, not one word was spoken by anyone, but all was mentally understood, as in telepathy. I felt the most awesome peacefulness, joy and all in composure, unconditional love of being there, and I knew without a doubt that it was not the first time nor it would be the last time I would visit this place. I had a wonderful conversation with God. I will not tell you every last thing that happened or was said, but that which I felt was the most important. God gave me a choice. He told me I could come home if I wanted to, meaning I did not need to go back. I had completed what it was that I came to accomplish for this lifetime. But I requested to be sent back, because I knew that I still wanted to help my boys, as they were not yet adults and if I did not come back there would be no guiding force in their lives to help them survive. My family was very scattered and dysfunctional and there was no one at that time who would have helped them. Although it was very tempting to want to stay, the bottomline was that the love in my heart for these two beautiful souls I had given birth to was much greater, and so of course I did return."

Connie further writes "This experience gave me a profound understanding of the nature of not only our relationship to God but also why reincarnation is a truth. God never meant for us to try and learn or experience everything in one lifetime. This is some of what I remembered. Our spirit originated from God in heaven. It can never die, it is only changed during our spiritual journey. Let me interject here that this reminds me of a quote I am very fond of, but forgive me, I cannot remember the author's name. 'We are not human beings having a spiritual experience, we are spiritual beings having a human experience.' This makes perfect sense to me, for it is perfect truth."

Connie further adds, "when we die here on earth it is only a physical death. Our body of flesh, bone and blood is only a physical vessel created to contain our spirit and the body is all that ever dies. Our spirit can never die. At the time of physical death our spirit simply leaves the body and returns home to heaven along with our memories and our personality. Every lifetime on this earth is recorded. During each individual lifetime we choose a different subject-matter to work on. We will continue the reincarnation cycle until we have reached a certain level of attainment or enlightenment, one might say. Eventually we will not need to return again. At which time we may pursue other spiritual paths on other levels."

Claire Harner Lynos in her poem *Immortality* has beautifully summed up the thoughts of Connie:

Do not stand
by my grave and weep
I am not there,
I do not sleep.

I am the thousand winds that blow,
I am the diamond glints in the snow,
I am the sunlight on ripened grain,
I am the gentle autumn rain.
As you awake with mornings hush,
I am the swift up-flinging rush
of quiet birds in circling flight.
I am the day transcending night

Do not stand
by my grave, and cry,
I am not there,
I did not die.

Connie claims that she was not at all influenced by any previous outside knowledge before this death-experience that would have influenced her experience. "Before that time I had very little information about reincarnation or what it even meant. At the time all I understood was the Christian perspective of death. So I did not even consider reincarnation in my own spiritual journey then, and I certainly had not heard of any experience like my own."

Fortunately, I met another person with profound impact of death-experience. R. Paul Firnhaber from Colorado, U.S.A., told me about his death-experience when he met me in Eskopje, Macedonia this summer, where we were attending an International Congress on Rock Art. Later, he was kind enough to send me the following letter that I am presenting here in his own words:

In 1999 I experienced two near-death experiences and one clinical death-experience. The following is an account of these experiences and my notes on the recovery as well as a reflective note on how these experiences were integrated into my life.

Near-death experience 30 May 1999 The first near-death experience (NDE) in this sequence was the result of an automobile accident, very serious, where I was a passenger. I technically should have died in the accident and thought that I was dead. I experienced *a brilliant white surrounding light, absolute silence and no pain whatsoever,* even though I was severely injured with a concussion, severe facial lacerations and a separated shoulder which later required surgery. When I realized that I was not dead, that I had in fact survived, I was seriously disappointed. Since I had authentic near-death experiences previously, I did'nt feel I was/would be impacted seriously by the NDE. However, I was seriously impacted by my injuries and went quickly into therapy of various sorts, particularly in dealing with the chronic fatigue and pain I was experiencing.

Clinical death-experience 04 March 2000 I had shoulder surgery in a Denver hospital for repairing the damage sustained in the automobile accident. During the night after surgery, while still in the hospital, I had an overdose/adverse reaction of *morphine.* The result was the rendering of my respiratory musculature not capable of functioning, resulting in respiratory arrest, or clinical death. I was revived in about 12 to 15 minutes by teams of specialists, and was incubated with oxygen until I was past the effects of the morphine. I am still not aware of the many details, and oddly enough, don't recall any of the classic death or near-death experiences, other than I was very much aware of having died and brought back to life. I feel that even then I was aware of the fact that life would no longer be the same, that there would be shifts in attitudes, orientations to reality and life, the extent of which I was not aware of. I faced a similar situation on 06 March 2000, when I was overdosed with a painkiller, *percodan.*

Since that time I have been under the care of neurological specialists and neurotherapists. I was diagnosed as having post-traumatic stress disorder (PTSD) that continually nudged its way to traumatically induced fibromalgia. The main thrust of the therapy was re-experiencing and re-activating, via hypnosis, traumatic events (death and near-death experiences) in an attempt to re-entertain neural pathways that might eventually allow appropriate signals to the hippocampus so that inappropriate responses would be replaced. This was an extreme process, and with very slow progress over several year's time, I was able to process input data in a less damaging way.

What I learned from these experiences, and what, finally, signficant about them is:

(a) The neurochemistry of death and near-death experiences is becoming identified, described, understood and mapped.

(b) This process is apart and distinct from cognitive processes. No frontal-lobe activity is involved. It is not possible, therefore, to manipulate this activity via cognitive techniques (psychotherapy; one can't "talked" out of it); rather it must be accessed and manipulated via pre-sub, or unconscious levels of brain activity and functioning (ASC).

(c) Such techniques seem to be parallel to and consistent with the techniques and activities of traditional cultures who have in the past, and sometimes still utilize alternate states of consciousness (ASC) for healing and healing rituals. It seems clear that those people utilizing trance and meditative states to access and manipulate hidden dimensions of reality (the sacred) are involving themselves and utilizing the selfsame psycho-neuro mechanisms that are involved in going into and returning from death itself; or death and re-birth.

(d) Technically I should have died, several times, and remained dead. The brain damage I experienced was the result of beating death, sometimes our systems

> aren't designed to allow us to do, and if and when we do, there are consequences. Such consequences are fully natural, and are becoming, to science, predictable and describable.

During these experiences I had some of the classic near-death experiences: pure white light, absence of sound/noise, extreme peace and serenity, a singularity with the cosmos and all of life, and especially a deep regret in having come back. I did not have the classic "life-reviewed-before-my-eyes" experience; rather it was an acceptance and embracing of my life as having been OK. Perhaps the most profound, actually overwhelming experience, was (and still is) a radical release from any fear of death (it was a major disappointment to return). Further, a passion about the unknown, the sacred, (and obversely, a trivialization of and disdain for the mundane) and the willingness to take inordinate risks to pursue it, has created a continuing revolution in me and my life, which arises, I feel, from the realization of the ease and beauty of death.

What did Connie experienced was real death or a condition of Coma, faintness or stance or was it really a journey of her spirit to another world. It is against the law of nature that a person gets retrieved from death. Also in clinical death, the death of brain is essential. Once the brain dies the body cannot come to life again, it means what Connie or Paul experi-enced was a near-death experience. The journey of the spirit or soul, passing through the white light and meeting with Jesus and God face-to-face, for me it is nothing but a dream of Connie based on her belief and faith. Thus, Connie was not dead, it was a near-death experience, she was in coma, she was dreaming and she saw (or experienced as she says) what was in her mind and thoughts according to her faith and beliefs. For Connie, it was the journey of her soul or spirit from her body to the heavens where she met Jesus and God. It means that Connie was in a condition of stance in which the spirit of the person leaves his/her body and met other spirits in the cosmos. On the contrary, Paul's experience is quite different. For Paul "it was the major disappointment to return;" while Connie was happy to return rather she asked God to send her back. A classical and well-known experience was common to both, *they saw pure white light*. Also, Connie's faith in incarnation is based on her belief and not on her experience because she immediately returned to life. She or anyone, who believes in incarnation, could never provide acceptable evidence about his or her past life. In fact, it is the beauty and curiosity of this unsolved mystery that forced us to believe in life-after-death without which no religion could survive. It is yet to be seen that we — the intelligent human beings, created by God — have created the laws of accountability of our deeds on this earth, to be imposed after our death, or these laws are really part of the constitution of God. We shall never know about its credibility in our lifetime.

It is interesting that people from different religions, experienced and witnessed in their dreams or in coma/stance or during near-death situation only those events which are related to their beliefs and religion. It is why Connie saw Jesus in her coma, or stance-condition. Many people wrote about their near-death experiences or about their dreams while they were in coma. Each of them strictly relates to his/her own faith and religion. A Muslim will claim, he saw Mohammed, a Jew shall see Moses and a Hindu will claim he saw Kr̥ṣṇa or Rāma. We shall never find a Muslim claiming he saw Buddha or Jesus or Kr̥ṣṇa during his/her near-death experience or in dream or stance-condition. Thus, it is the story of each person's belief and faith. The belief is continued since times unknown.

We have seen the tombs of Pharos filled with all luxury items of life, with the hope one day they will come to life on this earth. We have also seen ancient graves and tombs filled with treasures for the future life. I myself have excavated several graves, tombs and burials in various parts of Saudi

Arabia and found gold, silver and other objects buried with the perished and decomposed bodies. We human beings are always blind in our faiths and beliefs and very sensitive about the truth of our religions. This blind faith and belief is the basis of all religions; no religion can survive without the belief in life-after-death. The belief in life-after-death is the blood stream and heart of all the religions. However, it is in the best interest of humanity and all civilizations to believe in life-after-death in any form or shape to protect and preserve human rights and our social values.

References

Andrews, C., 1984, *Egyptian Mummies*, Boston, Harvad University Press.

Fleming, S., *et al.*, 1980, *The Egyptian Mummy: Secrets and Science*, University Museum of the University of Pennsylvania.

Bowker, J., 1997, *The Oxford Dictionary of World Religions*, Oxford University Press, Oxford, New York.

Cousineau, P., 1994, *Soul an Archaeology*, Harper Collins, New York.

Curtis, Herbert, D., (1994), *Continuity, from the Los Angles Times*, 31 December, 1926.

Gibran, K., 1976, *The Prophet* (*on Death*), Alfred A. Knopf, New York.

Goring, R., Whaling, F., 1994, *Larousse Dictionary of Beliefs and Religions*, Larousse Kingfisher Chambers, New York.

Rosten, L., 1975, *Religions of America* (*Fement and Faith in an Age of Crisis*), Simon and Schuster, New York.

Rumi, Jalal-uddin, (1207-75), *When I Have Sacrificed My Angel Soul.*

Socrates, *The Phaedo.*

6

Death in Sūfīs

Ahmed Sageer Inam Shastri

SUFISM is the name of good behaviour, as per the teachings of Holy *Koran*. There are five foundations of Islam, i.e., *tauheed*, (*kalmā*), *namāẓ*, *roẓa*, *haj* and *ẓakat*, and four major sources of Islamic knowledge to be practised in socio-religious life. They are (1) *Koran*, (2) *Hadīth*, (3) *Fiqaḥ*, and (4) *Qayas*.

Sufism means the belief and practices of Islam and soft and polite social behaviour with pure and honest heart and mind. Islam expects every Muslim to show Sufism (*Tasavvuf*) through his behaviour and actions. The person (Muslim) who follows Sufism is called "Sūfī."

Haẓrat Mohammad Bin Ali Bin Abutalib (RA) expressed that Sufism (*tasavvuf*) is the name of good behaviour. The status of *tasavvuf* may be measured on the basis of the degree of honesty and purity of good behaviour and habits (*Kashful Melyoob* — Urdu translation by Tufail Mohammad). There are two aspects of behaviour.

(i) Behaviour towards God; and

(ii) Behaviour towards human beings.

Haẓrat Murtayish (RA) has added one more type of behaviour, i.e., the Sūfī must not obey the (*Id'* and must control his desires which are to acquaint the teachings of the holy *Koran* and *Hadīth*).

The real Sūfī is one who successfully cleaned his heart from the sins and evil feelings. Sūfī makes his social contacts, interactions and social relations well accepted by the Islam and society.

According to Zunnon Misri (RA) a Sūfī speaks truth which never hurts the others as well as supported by the holy *Koran* and *Hadīth*. When he does not speak his gestures show that he has no desire of worldly things. His heart and mind remains free from the desire and needs of high standard of social life (example of Abu Bakr Siddique).

There is another view to understand Sufism, as a group of Muslim thinkers and believers consider it differently. However, there are four *muslak*s (thoughts) popular among the Muslims:

1. Hanafi — lead by Imam Abu Hanifa,
2. Maliki — lead by Imam Malik,
3. Shafayi — lead by Imam Shafayi,
4. Humbali — lead by Imam Ahmad Bin Humbal.

All of the followers believe in any one of the following ways of approach and call themselves as under:

1. Naqshbandī — (Khwaja Nehakuddin bin Mohammad Naqsh Band),
2. Chishtī (Khwaja Moinuddin Chishtī),
3. Qadirī (Sheikh Mohinuddin Abdul Qadir Jeelani),
4. Suharwardi (Sheikh Sahabuddin Suharwardi).

Sufism is a way of prayer and practise of Islamic views. They believe in no way of sophistication in performing the religious activities. The extreme of Sufism is an expression of their love to *Allāh* (the Almighty), Mohammad (PBUH), other prophets, Ghans, Walīs without any systematic approach or restrictions. They pray in a free and frank manner as they desire, and neither observe the systematic ways of prayers nor restrict to the following basic aspects of Islam such as *namāẓ, roẓa, haj* and *ẓakat* except *tauheed* (*kalmā*).

According to Islamic scholars there are three types of Sūfīs:

(1) Sūfī : The Sūfī is a person who is well dedicated to Islam and devotes his life for God and Soul. He must be free of sins, evils and unwanted desires.

(2) Mutsavvuf : The person trying to gain the qualities of dedication and behaviour of Sūfī, who wants to control his unwanted desires and *Id* as well as willing to purify his heart, is called Mutsavvuf.

(3) Mustasoof : There are persons who wish to enjoy luxurious socio-economic life. He wants to satisfy all his desires and needs without any socio-religious restriction. For this purpose he poses himself as a "Sūfī."

There is a systematic organization in the Sufism:

(1) Ghans (Mukhdoom) — Chief 1 in number,

(2) Aktab — 70 in number and out of them there is one Head called as Kutubul Aktab,

(3) Abdāl — 40 in number,

(4) Walī — 500 in number,

(5) Awtad — thousands (no limit of number).

Basically it is believed and followed in Sufism that the above structure of organization of Sūfīs runs the world systematically. They are placed in certain geographical areas according to their hierarchical status, to look after the people residing therein, without consideration of religion, caste or creed. None of the members of the organization retires but after the death of one, the other one will replace. In certain circumstances anyone may be transferred or replaced by another one.

Similarly, Haẓrat Huyveri, also indicates that the spirit of religion is obeying the teachings of God, extended through the holy *Koran* and *Hadīth*, with full confidence, devotion, love and dedication, which is in fact *tasavvuf*.

Haẓrat Abul Hasan highlighted that *tasavvuf* is not a name of particular physical appearance but it is the name of purity of mind and heart as well as the real obedience to God.

On the basis of the above discussion, we can understand that Sūfīs are the followers of Islam, not by words, physical actions, gestures and behaviour but by purity of heart and mind too.

No doubt, there is no concept of life and death among the Sūfīs, other than the concept of death in Islam.

Concept of Death

Tauheed (*kalmā*), *namāẓ*, *roẓa*, *haj* and *ẓakat* are five basic foundations/components of Islam. The holy *Koran* is a book of messages extended to the people by Almighty — *Allāh* (God) through his last messenger Mohammad (PBUH). Islam is the entire way of life. Messages indicated in *Koran* are reliable, believable and beyond any doubt. The teachings of *Koran* are not only for faithful Muslims but for the entire mankind. Every aspect of human life is clearly mentioned and clarified in the holy *Koran* and other related sacred books.

There are four sources of knowledge to be enacted in social and religious life:

(a) *Koran* — Messages by *Allāh* (God).

(b) *Hadīth* — Practice and behaviour of Mohammad (PBUH).

(c) *Fiqaḥ* — Explanations based on teachings of *Koran*.

(d) *Qayas* — Explanation given by the Islamic scholars on the matters not explained under the above three but in the light of *Koran* and *Hadīth*.

The concept of life and death are very well clarified in the above informative Islamic documents.

There are a number of verses (*surā*) in the holy *Koran* where indications about life, death, day of judgement, hell and garden (heaven) are given, such as *surā*s *Al Imran, Al Nisa, Al Ibrahim, Ambia, Unkaboot, Al Inam, Nahal, Nawaya Aala, Taha* and *Jasia.*

Here I wish to quote from *sura Al Imran* (III.185) "Every soul shall have a taste of death" (the soul will not die, but the death of the body will give a taste of death to the soul. When the soul separates from the body, the soul will then know that this life was but a probation. And seeming inequalities will be adjusted finally on the Day of Judgement. And only on the day of judgement shall you be paid your full recompense. Only he who is saved far from the fire and admitted to the garden would attain the object (of life), for the life of this world is but goods and chattels of deception).

According to Islam, "no one can escape from death", as indicated in *Dura Ambia* (XXI.35) and also in *sura Unkaboot* (XXIX.57). Every soul shall have a taste of death: and we test you by evil and by good by way of trial to us must ye return, and, "Every soul shall have a taste of death. In the end to us shall ye be brought back."

As a result of death, body will die but the soul is immortal. "Nor can a soul die; except by God's leave. The term being fixed as by writing. If any does desire a reward in this life we shall give it to him, and if any does desire a reward in the hereafter, we shall give it to him. And swiftly shall we reward those that (serve us with) gratitude" (*sura Imran*, III.145).

Everyone who is born by the grace of God will die and then will be gathered for the Day of Judgement, of course the soul will never die. It is emphasized in *sura Waqaya* (LVI.60-61, 83, 87) "We have decreed Death to be your common lot, we are not to be frustrated. From changing your Forms and creating you (again) in (Forms) that ye know not."

Further indicated in *sura Iram* (VI.36) "There who will raise them up, then will they be turned into him."

"After the judgement the sinners/non-believers will go to hell and believers will be sent to garden." (*Sura* Taha, XX.75-76).

God is highlighted in *sura Jasia* (XLV.26), "It is God who gives you life, then gives you death, then He will gather you together for the Day of Judgement about which there is no doubt: but most men do not understand."

However, we may discuss about the concept of death in the light of indications in the holy *Koran* and eight characteristics of *tasavvuf* as pointed out by Haẓrat Junaid:

(i)	Shakhawat	:	As Haẓrat Ibrāhim donated all of his belongings and sacrificed his son in the name of God.
(ii)	Raza	:	As Haẓrat Ismail obeyed his father Ibrāhim and desire of God and presented himself for sacrifice.
(iii)	Sabr	:	As Haẓrat Ayub love lore a painful life and lost his family in crisis/ trouble.
(iv)	Isharat	:	As Haẓrat Ẓakaria stopped talking for a long time and managed his living without expressing a single word but indications.
(v)	Ghurbut	:	As Yahya who lived in crucial economic conditions and loneliness.

(vi)	Lebase Sauf (Gudrī)	:	As Haẓrat Moosa wore woollen dress *gudrī.* As Haẓrat Isā migrated to unknown place, only with a comb and a cup which he had thrown in the way.
(vii)	Saiyahat	:	
(viii)	Fuqr	:	As Haẓrat Mohammad (PBUH) lived in severe poverty though God offered him a Treasure.

The above characteristics of Sūfīs show that the real Sūfī is the person who must have the qualities to sacrifice, obedience to God, thankfulness to God in every condition and must be able to control and manage unwanted physical and mental desires. He must be happy and satisfied in the poorest socio-economic condition. He must wear only ordinary clothes (*gudrī*), travel without any facility for the sake of religion and human welfare and prefer to live in poverty and must not accept the luxurious items, even if a treasure is offered by the God.

It means that Sūfīs are least interested in worldly things. The objective of ones life in this world is to get the result of deeds in the life after death. He never expects any return of his good, honest and selfless behaviour and deeds in this world but wants to gain for the everlasting life after death. A Sūfī believes that the real life starts after the death. So he always welcomes the death at any stage or time.

7

Christian Belief in Resurrection

George Rajmohan

RESURRECTION of Jesus is the central faith-content of all Christian churches and denominations. The resurrection of Jesus is recorded in all the Gospels, Mathew 28, 1-8; Mark 16, 1-8; Luke 24, 1-12; and John 20, 1-10. Luke puts down the resurrection-narrative very graphically.

> Very early on Sunday morning the women went to the tomb, carrying the spices they had prepared. They found the stone rolled away from the entrance to the tomb, so they went in; but they did not find the body of the Lord Jesus. They stood there puzzled about this, when suddenly two men in bright shining clothes stood by them. Full of fear, the women bowed down to the ground, as the men said to them. "Why are you looking among the dead for one who is alive?" He is not here; he has been raised. Remember what he said to you while he was in Galilee: "The Son of Man must be handed over to sinful men, be crucified, and three days later (he will) rise to life."
>
> Then the women remembered his words, returned from the tomb and told all these things to the eleven disciples and all the rest. The women were Mary Magdalene, Johanna and Mary, the mother of James; they and other women with them told these things to the apostles. But the apostles thought that what the women said was nonsense and they did not believe them. But Peter got up and ran to the tomb; he bent down and saw the linen wrappings but nothing else. Then he went back home amazed at what had happened. — Luke 24, 1-12

Anyone trying to understand the Christian faith in resurrection must know a couple of important things. First of all it should be noted that the resurrection of Jesus in fact triggered a worldwide religious movement almost soon after the incident, proclaiming love and hope on the face of a horrific happening of a crucified man named Jesus. Roman capital punishment included crucifixion of the condemned criminals. His own people condemned Jesus as a heretic and troublemaker. But he becomes the centre of a religious revolution. Resurrection was the central theme of the apostles and his disciples in their preaching of this new religious sect.

Secondly, resurrection was not understood by any one as a resuscitation of the body of the crucified Jesus, rather a new reality of life and joy and a hope beyond compare for his believers. Resurrection became the central message of their faith-proclamation, reconciling the most horrific event in the history to a most sublime hope of human beings on earth. The suffering and death of Jesus is a historical event but his resurrection becomes an eschatological faith event (faith in a glorious future life). It is only people of faith who experienced the risen Lord, and even then, sometimes with great hesitation and overcoming of doubts. This faith far exceeded all the doubts and prevailed over for the centuries that followed.

St. Paul in his letter to the Corinthians hinges this faith in the resurrection of Jesus to the resurrection of everyone who believes. "The truth is that Christ has been raised from death as the guarantee that those who sleep in death will also be raised." (1 Cor. 15.20) Resurrection of all who die in faith is the core belief among the Christians. This belief in resurrection, one should not forget, was not part and parcel of the belief of the Jewish religion, which was the religion of Jesus. How did then this idea become prominent in Christianity?

Puzzle of the Life-after

Death is a reality of life and the life-after-death a puzzle. Why do we die at all? The question becomes poignant on the face when someone of our own dies. We die because we are mortal. Our bodies disintegrate for the same reason as our clothes are worn out or the old chairs and tables break and rust. Death is the law of matter. All material things wear out and disintegrate. Stars die! this applies to man also?

From the very day human beings became self-conscious, the desire to overcome death became an aspiration of man. Elaborate rituals and funeral ceremonies were conducted in almost every civilization, primitive or modern indicating the belief in a life-after. Hope prevails in man even on the face of death. A nihilistic attitude to life is a rare and exceptional phenomenon in human life. A life-after seems to be the norm in most cultures. The oriental religions mostly believe in reincarnation while the Semitic religions have the belief in resurrection. In any case, belief in the resurrection of the body as it is believed, is unique to Christianity.

Idea of Reincarnation

The idea of reincarnation is not exactly an oriental position on life. In *Timaeus* of Plato — an ancient Greek Philosopher — we read:

> The Demiurge created as many souls as there are stars, and then laid down the laws by which their destinies would be governed:
>
> At the first birth, the conditions of all souls will be equal so that there will be no disadvantaged among them, entering into Time and distributed throughout the universe, these souls will take on the nature most capable of honouring the gods.
>
> However, human nature being dual, superiority must be deemed to reside in the virile (i.e., male) sex. Once souls have been implanted in bodies, and the person's actions have resulted in either losses or gains . . . he who has lived right will mount towards the particular star assigned to him to dwell there in a condition of happiness that conforms to the state of his soul. However, he who has failed the test will be reborn again, changing his nature for that of a woman. If, in this new nature, the soul

> does not cease and desist from malice, it will be reincarnated continuously into animal bodies acording to the nature of its vice. Through such continued metamorphoses, it will never see the penalties it must suffer. Having made known to souls these dispositions of the laws by which their destinies would be governed definitely not fore-knowing the malice to which any of them might become prey — the Demiurge then thrust the created souls into Time, distributing them throughout the earth and the moon.
>
> — Jowett's tr., *The Dialogues of Plato*, vol. III, p. 461

The passage is comparable to the *Chāndogya Upaniṣad* (5.10.3-7). According to these ancient texts, rebirth is the consequence of one's actions. Male birth is superior to female birth. Life-after is determined by one's own action. Rebirth ideas are found in many tribal religions of both India and Africa. It should be noted here that the idea of rebirth is comparable to the rhythm of nature we observe in day-to-day life. The concept of rebirth upholds the close affinity between man and nature. It is certainly a theory of after-life that is believed by so many civilizations.

The ideas of rebirth contain a dichotomous view of body-soul relationship. Soul is reborn and the body disintegrates. Soul is eternal but the body is mortal. Soul is pure while the body is impure. Each rebirth carries a new body. The real self does not involve the body. For Plato, body is a prison house. Virtuous life is one that shuns the body. Release of the body is liberation. The importance of action or *karma* as an entity that determines the future life does not admit exceptions. Some of the strict oriental positions of *karma* does not even permit the grace of the divine in salvation! Salvation is the final release of the soul from the cycle of birth and death. And this one can achieve by good actions and overcoming the desires of the body.

Idea of Resurrection

The idea of resurrection is in fact quite different from the theory of rebirth or reincarnation. Resurrection establishes not only the immortality of the soul alone, but also of the body. It admits grace of God as a fact of our immortality. Man and nature, according to this position, are not separated. Body and soul are integral part of the reality of human being. In the Nicene Creed of the Church, every Christian repeats almost everyday in his profession of faith: "I believe in the resurrection of the body and life everlasting." Resurrection as it is believed in the Christian churches believe bodily resurrection. Body is not a prison house or defiling material of life. Body is the vehicle of salvation and an integral part of the human person. Human being is a composite of body and soul. Body and soul are not two entities in the human being, but two dimensions of the same reality.

This anthropological vision marks a vast difference between the Christian faith in resurrection and the belief in reincarnation or rebirth. In both these beliefs moral behaviour is emphasized for the realization of the final goal of salvation but with the difference that the grace of the Divine is emphasized in the belief in resurrection. The anthropological differences in the concepts of body-soul relationship are clearly evident in the after-life concept of Christianity and religions that believe in reincarnation. Although both the views — resurrection as well as reincarnation hold the immortality of the soul, the fundamental difference is the destiny of the body, the nature and the cosmos itself.

The dichotomous conception of body and soul had disastrous consequences in the history of civilizations. Christianity itself, influenced by the ideas of Plato and his Christian disciple, St. Augustine, could not accept the positive aspects of the physical life. Body was considered in such negation that it was believed that it should be subjugated, controlled, denied and overcome for the City of God! This negative understanding of the human body is also a heritage of the Church that condoned the torturous inquisitions, burning of the witches and sadistic spiritual paths of abnegation and asceticism, condemnation of everything other than European as heathen, and women as inferior to man. The overall picture of this distortion continued in the Churches until recently and its remnants are visible even today!

It is the split notion of human person that is challenged by the resurrection ideals. The Christian notion of resurrection glorifies the human as both spiritual and material and hopes the overcoming of death in a new earth and new heaven. "I believe in the resurrection of body," is a new cosmic vision. Human person is hitherto considered the image of god immortal and dignified, his labour as the creative fulfilment of the cosmic plan of God. We are the "spirit in the world," (Karl Rahner) fulfilling the destiny of the Universe. In man, matter and spirit get the final realization. Man is not a static creature of God, a servant, but a creator himself, sharing the creative plan of God. He is a becoming. He is still in the making. Human being is still evolving to perfection, his final destiny and fulfilment.

It is this that happened in the case of Jesus on that fateful Saturday night. He rose from the dead. His body attained a new dimension, a transcendental dimension, overcoming the limitation of space and time. The joy of resurrection is the fulfilment of the cosmic plan of God. It is bliss. "Peace be with you," tells He to His frightened friends. Walking straight into the closed room of the disciples, He strengthens their belief.

> Suddenly the Lord himself stood among them and said to them, "Peace be with you." They were terrified, thinking that they were seeing a ghost. But he said to them, "Why are you alarmed? Look at my hands and my feet and see that it is I myself. Feel me and you will know, for a ghost does not have flesh and bones, as you can see I have."
>
> He said this and showed them his hands and his feet. They still could not believe, they were so full of joy and wonder.
>
> — Luke 24.36-42

Resurrection is the most wonderful deed of a loving God to a mortal humanity. It is the most joyful event of Christian faith. The consequence of this belief is greater reverence to the human person even after death. Death is not the end of life but the beginning of an everlasting life in God.

Part II
Science and Society

8

Extinction
Geological View of Death

Pratul Kumar Saraswati

Introduction

DEATH, an inevitable truth, acts at different levels, some perceptible and others imperceptible at the scale of human life-span. A cell dies, an individual dies, a population dies, a species dies, and so also the genus and the higher taxonomic categories of life. The definition of death, if at all there is any, for the living animals cannot be applied to the fossil forms in the geologic records. The death of a species is called "extinction." According to the *Oxford Dictionary*, the word "extinction" is a noun of the adjective "extinct," which means no longer burning, quenched, having died out, obsolete. Some call it a reduction in the geographic range of a species to zero (Stearn and Carroll, 1989). Even though the early naturalists had observed that some of the fossil forms were no longer seen in the present world, until late in the eighteenth-century, extinction of species was not a widely accepted view. It was considered that such creatures were living in unexplored areas of the earth. In 1786, George Cuvier stated that there is no possibility of mammoths having been overlooked, and therefore they are extinct. This view was well-received and soon extinction of many species was considered valid (Stanley, 1999). Charles Darwin in his seminal work in 1859 discussed both about the origin and extinction of species. Contrary to the catastrophist-geologists of his times, Darwin did not believe in Noah's Flood, and instead argued for "species gradually disappearing, one after another, first from one spot, then from another, and finally from the world." Like an individual organism, species too lived for a particular span of time. In comparison with a short life-span of humans, the average life-span of species is estimated by palaeontologists to be about three million years. To understand extinction ("death") of species, one needs to know the origin ("birth") of species. The two are complementary to each other. Origin is to extinction what the life is to death. Without life there is no death and without origin there is no extinction. There cannot be a better example to illustrate this concept than the fossil records of more than 500 million years of the evolutionary history of our planet.

Speciation and Extinction

To a biologist, a species is a set of actually or potentially interbreeding population. There are practical problems in applying this concept to fossil specimens and, therefore, palaeontologists base their definition on morphological criteria. The formation of new species is called speciation. The Darwinian concept of speciation visualizes a gradual transformation of one species into another, detected by gradual change in morphological attributes. This is called phyletic gradualism. In such a process there is no increase in the number of co-existing species. Most biologists do not consider this as speciation and call it phyletic transformation (Raup, 1991: 210). Eldredge and Gould (1972) pointed out that fossil species remained in stable (equilibrium) condition for millions of years and punctuated by the sudden introduction of new species that formed in some peripherally isolated area. They called this process the punctuated equilibrium. Such a process is also in conformity with the modern genetic viewpoint. Natural populations are large reservoir of interbreeding individuals and their combined genes constitute a gene-pool. If a novel mutation of advantage under natural selection appears in some individuals of this population, it will soon hybridize out by diluting the genes that control the mutants. Therefore it is critical that such mutations occur in peripherally isolated population so that the unusual genes become dominant in the population. This will lead to formation of a new species if the descendents find it advantageous. In this process of allopatric speciation, there is splitting or branching of an evolutionary line and thereby an increase in the number of co-existing species. Many palaeontolgists now consider gradual change to be rare in stratigraphic record but there are good examples of this type in certain groups documented well by micro-palaeontoligists.

The problem of species identification in palaeontology is very much at the core of the concept of species extinction. In a gradually evolving populations, the change in morphological traits are so wide between the beginning and the end that it is pertinent to subdivide the lineage, howsoever arbitrary the division may be. In such a transformation of one species into another, the parent one is considered to become extinct as the new species is evolved by anagenesis. Many palaeontologists, however, are not in favour of subdividing an anagenetic lineage and suggest that species are formed only by branching events. Simpson called this evolutionary species. This concept has problems in anagenetic lineages where the end-members are distinctly different. Between the two above-stated concepts of species the former conceptualizes the death of a species by its slow transformation into a new form of life. The extinction of this kind is referred to as phyletic extinction or pseudo-extinction. There is no loss of number of species in this case. The second kind of extinction is the true extinction or terminal extinction wherein a species lineage becomes extinct. Here there is a loss of species. The fossil records of both kinds are observed.

Why Do Species Get Extinct?

We can say with very little certainty why organisms get extinct. There are several plausible factors that cause extinction of species. It includes competition and predation from other organisms, changes in the ambient physico-chemical environments and chance events of local, regional or global scales. The chance events may be hurricanes, forest fires and tidal waves affecting local populations of a species or it may be sea-level change, volcanism or exra-terrestrial impact, leading to extinction of regional to global populations. The chance events act indiscriminately on all kinds of life-forms while the physico-chemical and biological parameters are believed to affect those forms that fail to adapt to the changing environment. The adaptive failure as a cause of extinction has been debated in recent years. A careful analysis of the anatomical features of fossil species of the famous Burgess Shale horizon of British Columbia led palaeontologists to conclude that there is no evidence to link evolutionary success with better anatomical design. As Gould (1989: 239) puts it, "We do not know for sure that the Burgess decimation was a lottery. But we have no evidence that the winners enjoyed adaptive superiority. . . ." The question has been raised whether extinction is due to bad gene or bad luck. Van Valen (1973) carried this debate further and proposed a controversial view that the probability of extinction of a short-lived species is the same as that of a long-lived survivor species. It has several implications. If one views evolution as producing progressively improving species so that those who survived were better adapted, then the long-lived species should have a lower probability of extinction. If evolution produced more specialized species then the long-lived species would be more vulnerable to extinction. Neither of these is true, according to Van Valen.

A statistical analysis of the extinction records suggests that the marine invertebrates of the phanerozoic time (the last 550 million years) became extinct at a rate of 2.0 to 4.5 families per million years. Against this average figure, called background extinction, there stands five major periods where 10 to 20 families became extinct every million years. These exceptionally high extinction rates are called "mass-extinction" and occurred during Ordovician, Devonian, Permian, Triassic and Cretaceous periods of the geological time-scale. Some palaeontologists argue for the use of term "mass killing" in place of "mass extinction." The most debated and popular mass extinction is the Cretaceous extinction that occurred 65 million years ago and that led to the demise of the mighty dinosaurs, among others. This extinction is believed to have occurred due to an extra-terrestrial impact. A further statistical analysis of the extinction data led David Raup and associates to conclude that the pulses of extinctions in the evolutionary history of life are spaced at a periodicity of about 26 million years. The astronomers came up with an explanation that the companion star, Nemesis, of the Sun disturbs the orbit of the comets every 26 million years, causing showers of the comets on the earth. There is a belief that we are passing through the phase of sixth mass extinction. Unlike the past extinctions caused by natural phenomena, the present crisis is considered to be the result of human interference. Wilson (1992) estimates that in rain forests 27,000 species are getting extinct each year due to reduction in forest area. If we consider this rate of extinction, the sixth mass extinction will be the severest of all the mass extinctions on this planet. And it would be unique in having the birth of a species, the *Homo sapiens*, as a cause of most devastating extinction ever recorded in the evolutionary history of life.

To conclude, the death of species incorporates three concepts: (i) transformation from one form to the other, (ii) failure to adapt to changing environment, and (iii) killing by natural or extra-terrestrial processes. The recent developments in the field of molecular biology to clone the extinct animals may raise another dimension to the death of species: "do the species ever die?"

References

Darwin, C.R., 1859, *On the Origin of species by means of Natural Selection*, J. Murray, London.

Eldredge, N., and S.J. Gould, 1972, "Punctuated Equilibria — An Alternative to Phyletic Gradualism," in Schopf, T.J.M. (ed.), *Models in Paleobiology*, Freeman, San Francisco, pp. 82-115.

Gould, S.J., 1989, *Wonderful Life — The Burgess Shale and the Nature of History*, W.W. Norton and Co., New York.

Raup, D.M., 1991, *Extinction — Bad Genes or Bad Luck?*, W.W. Norton and Co., New York.

S.M. Stanley, 1999, *Earth System History*, W.H. Freeman and Co., New York.

Stearn, C. and R. Carroll, 1989, *Paleontology — The Record of Life*, John Wiley and Sons, New York.

Wilson, E.O., 1992, *The Diversity of Life*, Penguin Books, London.

9

Death in Biological System

Madan Mohan Chaturvedi

IF life is a reality, the death is an eternal truth. Organisms exist because they are alive. But if they have to evolve, they must die as well. The perpetuation and evolution are hallmarks of the existence of living systems. Death is an inevitable process. Anything that is born has to die. This looks like a philosophical statement and it is beyond the scope of discussion in Biology. However, this statement can easily be understood with the *Thermodynamic Concept of Entropy*.

Philosophy within Biology

Thermodynamics is a branch of science that deals with energy transformation. It also defines the interaction of a *system* with its *surroundings*. System plus surroundings together are called *universe*. There are *three types of thermodynamic systems*: *Closed* (which can only exchange the energy and not the matter with its surroundings), *Open* (which can exchange both energy and matter with its surroundings), and *Isolated* (which can neither exchange energy nor the matter with its surroundings). Living systems are thermodynamically open systems that maintain a continuous flux of energy and matter with its surroundings. In this context the existence of living system can never be understood if it is studied in isolation.

Let us bring one more thermodynamic term into consideration: that is the Entropy. Entropy (or state within) defines the randomness of a system or its surroundings. A system, which is well defined has an order in it, has low entropy. A system at low entropy would exist as long as it is somehow able to increase the entropy of its surroundings such that the entropy of system and surroundings keep increasing. The moment this rule is not followed, the system disintegrates and dies. What happens to the disintegrated system, and which system would be most stable and would not die, can be understood from the discussions in the following paragraphs.

The disintegrated system, now with high entropy after death, becomes part and parcel of a system that is an isolated one and is the most stable. But to have a most stable system at highest entropy, the system should not have any order or shape. This is very difficult to imagine in terms of West-looking (so-called modern) science. But it is very easy to understand if explained according to Indian philosophy of *nirākāra Brahman.* In order to understand the concept of *nirākāra Brahman* in terms of entropy, it is essential that the entropy be understood not simply as randomness, but as a state of probability. Defining entropy as randomness gives a wrong notion of disorderness. A system that has an order and hence a low entropy would have a very low probability of being found by chance at more than one place at any given time. Contrary to this, a system with high or maximum entropy does not have any shape as a result, but would have maximum probability of being found at any place at any given time. Hence, the *nirākāra Brahman* would never die, would not have any shape, and would have a very high probability of being found everywhere. Hence, a living system dies not because of a disease or as a result of some stochastic processes, but it is destined to die to become part and parcel of most stable system, from where more and newer kind of unstable system can be created, if needed.

Death — An Equilibrium

Since, according to biochemists, life processes are nothing

but a sum of complex chemical reactions, let us understand the life in the form of a chemical reaction. If A is converted to B, it is depicted as A — B. This reaction would occur till the Free Energy Change (ΔG — *a term which includes both the entropy and the enthalpy*) of the reaction is negative (or *endergonic*, means the reaction has the capacity to do work on the surrounding). When the reaction ceases to do work on the surrounding, the free energy change of the reaction becomes zero and the reaction comes to equilibrium. Such reaction is depicted as $A = B$. Hence, a reaction occurs till it attains the equilibrium. Therefore, the reactions in a living system would occur till they come to an equilibrium and when the system loses its capacity to work then at that point it is said to be dead. *Hence, death is the equilibrium of life, and life exists to come to its equilibrium.*

Biology of Cell-Death

The so-called modern science has only recently started understanding the importance of death in living systems. We are not even close to understand why and how the organisms die but some beginning has been made in understanding how does a cell (the building block of a living system) die. Too much as well as too little of cell-death, both result into disease-conditions. The process of cell-death has been defined as of two types: the Necrotic cell-death and the Apoptotic Cell-Death. The necrotic cell-death is accidental and unprogrammed and if it occurs its results into a lot of side-reactions. Opposite to this, the apoptotic cell-death is a programmed one, and it occurs in a controlled manner. Millions of cells are dying in our body everyday but there occurs no side-effect and we do not even feel it. Both body sculpting during embryonic development and maintenance of homostasis in adulthood require apoptotic cell-death.

The growing importance of understanding of mechanism of cell-death is evident from the fact that the Nobel Foundation Committee awarded during 2002 Nobel Prize in Physiology and Medicine to three scientists (Sydney Brenner, John Sulston, and Robert Horvitz) who contributed immensely to our present concept of programme cell-death. According to them, every cell is destined to die as it is born, loaded with destructive machinery made up of *proteros* called *caspases.* (One of the Scientists from U.S.A. who is of Indian origin, who discovered a caspase, called it as Yama). However, this machinery is kept under strict control. There are basically *four steps* in the process of programme cell-death: *Decision, Induction, Execution* and *Disposal.* A lot of information is available at Induction and Execution steps, but very little is known regarding decision and disposal. However, as the field of programme cell-death is growing very fast, it is expected that more information and better understanding of these steps will soon follow.

10

Science of Death

Lavina Chaubey

DEATH of a person scientifically occurs in two stages:

(1) Clinical death wherein life ceases in the body as a whole, signified by cessation of vital functions of the body, and

(2) Molecular death, which is loss of life in the component parts of the body, generally occurs and complete within 3-4 hours after the clinical death.

The need to make a distinction between the two is important so that one may know when exactly to proceed for cremation or burial and for the purpose of transplantation of organs.

Clinical death may occur due to the cessation of functions of the three vital structures. First is the brain, which fails to function due to a variety of reasons and manifests as coma. Secondly, failure of the heart which manifests as syncope or fainting. Third is asphyxia caused by the failure of function of lungs which cuts the oxygen supply to important areas of the body. All the three factors may cause death individually or jointly and are called the proximate or immediate cause of death. However, there has to be an underlying cause for these factors, and such causes must be clearly stated wherever required.

Signs of Death

It is important to recognize each and every sign of death for the purpose of averting dangerous mistakes. They are usually divided into three categories depending on the time period.

IMMEDIATE SIGNS

These usually are the signs of clinical death:

(a) Insensibility and loss of voluntary power to move, associated with a total loss of EEG (electroencephalogram) incessantly for a period of five minutes.

(b) Cessation of circulation, that is, when a careful auscultation of the heart with a stethoscope reveals no heart sounds for a continuous period of five minutes it becomes an acceptable evidence of death.

(c) Cessation of respiration. This again must be complete and continuous to cause death.

EARLY SIGNS

These are consistent with molecular or cellular death and occur 3-4 hours after the clinical death.

Cooling of the body

During life, there is a balance between heat production and heat loss. After death, heat production stops and the body loses heat till it is in equilibrium with the temperature of its surroundings. The progressive fall in temperature is one of the most important early signs of death, the amount of cooling indicating the approximate time elapsed since death.

Changes in the eye

The clear, glistening appearance of the cornea is lost and it becomes cloudy. This is usually associated with dilatation of the pupil which does not constrict.

Changes in the skin

(a) Due to loss of circulation the skin becomes pale and sallow, looses its translucency and elasticity.

(b) Discolouration or staining of skin due to accumulation of fluid blood in dependent parts of the body.

Changes in the Muscle

(a) *Primary Relaxation:* Immediately after death in ordinary circumstances, there is relaxation of the general muscular tone leading to drooping of the lower jaw, sinking of eye balls in their sockets, dilated pupils, soft and flabby muscles, flexible joints with no resistance and the sphincters relax.

(b) *Rigor Mortis:* After a period of primary relaxation of the muscles they become rigid (Rigor — rigidity, Mortis — of death) due to chemical changes involving proteins of the musclel fibers.

(c) *Secondary Relaxation:* When rigor mortis disappears the muscle become soft and flaccid again.

LATE SIGNS

These are consistent with decaying of the body. However, a modification of the process may lead to:

(a) Mummification

(b) Adipocere formation.

Here it is important to state that all the signs of death are not foolproof evidences and can be altered by a variety of factors.

Therefore, it is important to look at the composite picture and take a second opinion when in doubt.

11

Death in Āyurveda

K.H.H.V.S.S. Narasimha Murthy
R.H. Singh

THE Indian word for death is *mṛtyu*, which means the loss of life (*prāṇa viyogaḥ*). According to the *Āyurveda*, that which keeps the body capable of discharging the life-activities effectively and continuously is *prāṇa*. There are twelve types of *prāṇa: agni, soma, vāyu, sattva, raja, tama*, five *indriyās* and *bhūtas*. They are located in ten different places (*daśa prāṇayatanam*) namely, two *śaṁkhas*, three *marma sthānas* (*śiro, rāśi, hṛdaya*), *kaṇṭha, rakta, śukra, ojas* and *gudā*. The other Sanskrit terms for *mṛtyu* are *pañcata, kalādharmuḥ, diṣṭantaḥ, pralaya, ātyayaḥ, antaḥ, nāśa, maraṇam, nidhanam, pacatṛvam, mṛtam, mṛti, naidhanem, samkhya, kālu, paralokagamana, dīrgha nidrā, nimīlanam, astam, āśāśanam, bhūmilabam, nipātaḥ, vilaya, atyayikam*, and *apyayaḥ*.

According to *Āyurveda*, life, i.e., the activity of *prāṇa* is the combination of *śarīra, indriya, sattva* and *ātmā* in an uninterrupted manner. The break in this union is known as *mṛtyu* (non-*āyu*). The body (*śarīra*) is one of the components of life (*āyu*); it is made up of five elements (*pañcamahābhūtas*). In the form of *doṣa, dhātu* and *mala* the elements discharge and function in body. When the union breaks down changes take place. First the *ātmā* (soul) separates and disappears; next, the function of *indriya* stops (*cetana* becomes *acetana*) and then the body starts decomposing to its basic constituents, that is the five elements. The process of degradation and decomposition is called *pañcatva* which is a synonym of *mṛtyu*.

The other synonym is *pralaya*, which means the phenomenal change is happening in the body as death occurs. If the deeds of previous life (*daiva*) are more powerful than those of the present they get nullified and the vice versa can also be seen. The unsuitable and harmful activity (*pāpa karma*) gives its effect in the form of diseases. Sometimes the disease becomes uncontrollable (*asādhya*) and kills the patient. All the measures taken to treat the disease fail. This shows that the *daiva* is more powerful than the gains of the deeds (*puraskāra*). In the process, the soul (*ātman*) is relieved from the bondage of life (*āyu*), it merges into the Great Soul (*paramātmā*). This is called *laya* or *pralaya*. Ultimately the *āyu* (union of body, organs, goodness and soul) becomes *anāyu* (non-life) or death (*mṛtyu*). The word *maraṇam* also explains this phenomenon. The disjunction of the unity of mind (*manas*) and soul (*ātmā*) has been well-explained in Nyāya philosophy.

Āyurveda takes a holistic approach to treat the diseases and maintains the body of an individual. It mentions that there are one-hundred-and-one types of death located in one's body. Of these, one is called timely death (*kāla mṛtyu*) and all the rest are untimely (*akāla mṛtyu*). One can prevent untimely death by administering medicine (*auṣadha*) and such religious performances as *japa, homa, dāna,* etc.

Death in Other Life Sciences

The advancement of scientific inventions in different fields has brought a lot of change in understanding death. Once the philosophers, priests, lawyers and laymen defined death as complete stoppage of heart and respiratory functions. This thought has been changing due to scientific advancement in medical and other life sciences. A new branch of science has developed to study death, its types and medico-legal significances. It is called Thanatology.

The study of death is not only important for the medical purposes but also for the law. It is important to decide or identify the successor of the property for which it is necessary to note the death and its types and time, etc. The human organ transplantation has also led to the necessity of scrutinizing the phenomena of death. It has raised medical, ethical and legal questions concerning as to when to remove the organ from the donor. One has to remember that the organ must be removed at the earliest, after the donor has been declared dead. But it is difficult to decide when the artifical means be utilized. This has opened a new concept of the moment of death. There are two mechanisms of death, somatic and molecular death. The somatic death is that in which the irreversible cessation of functions of brain, heart and lungs results in complete loss of sensibility and ability to move the body. The molecular death is that in which the ultimate death of all cellular elements takes place. Thus, when a person's individual cell starts dying, it is called Cellular or Molecular death. This molecular death happens step by step in different cells at different times, after complete cessation of circulation of blood and respiration. The cells which die first are brain cells, within five minutes of cessation of circulation and respiration. After brain cells, muscle cells start dying by the end of the first hour of somatic death. It takes more hours of time for all muscle tissues to die. The cornea and blood cells remain alive for five hours after the cessation of circulation and respiration. The fibrous tissues die later. To put it in a nutshell, the organs or tissues which receive more blood supply during life, will die early in the absence of blood supply. Thus one can say that the cessation of circulation and respiration is not exactly death. Even after the stoppage of circulation there are tissues and organs surviving and they can be removed and transplanted immediately. This concept has opened a new type of death called Brain Death, whose symptoms and signs are:

1. deep unconsciousness with no response to external stimuli or internal need;
2. no chest movement, and no spontaneous breathing;
3. cessation of spontaneous cardiac rhythm without assistance;

4. no neurological reflexes;
5. bilateral dilatation and fixation of pupils;
6. flat iso-electric EEG;
7. no metabolic and endocrine disturbances, which can cause coma; and
8. no marked abnormality in serum electrolytes, acid-base balance and blood glucose.

Changes After Death

These are of three types:

Immediate changes: (1) stoppage of function of nervous system; (2) stoppage of respiration; and (3) stoppage of circulation. All these changes are nothing but symptoms and signs of Somatic Death.

Early changes: (1) facial pallor; (2) loss of elasticity of the skin with decrease in facial creases; (3) primary relation of muscles; (4) contact pallor and contact flattening; (5) changes in eye; (6) cooling of the body; (7) postmortem staining (lividity); and (8) rigor mortis or postmortem rigidity. These are changes that happen due to the Molecular Death.

Late changes: (1) putrefaction and ordinary decomposition; (2) adepocere change (a modified form of decomposition); and (3) mummification (another form of modified decomposition).

The ordinary decomposition can be understood as follows: It is a process by which the complex organic body-tissues break down into simpler inorganic compounds or elements. This is due to autolysis or otherwise due to the invasion of saprophytic micro-organisms which produce ferments. Step by step, changes in this process occur, namely discolouration of dead body, evolution of foul smelling gas, swelling of the dead body with gradual and total destruction of the different body parts.

The above explanation of the whole process is nothing but *pañcatva,* as explained by the *Āyurveda*. Thus, whatever the way one understands, the process of death (*mṛtyu*) is same.

Causes of Death

Āyurveda accepts the six basic causes of death and birth as follows:

1. ***Svabhāva*** means natural. This theory explains that everything happens due to Nature. It explains that the sharpness in thorns, multi-colouredness in animals and birds, sweetness in sugar cane, pungent taste in black pepper, etc., all are due to the Natural phenomenon only. So death is also a Natural phenomenon.

2. ***Īśvara*** means god or Supreme soul or force. This theory explains that all the creator of movable and immovable beings of this Universe and the determiner of entry and exit of being into *svarga* and *naraka* is the god. So death is also caused by god.

3. ***Kāla*** means time. This theory explains that the time is a causative factor for everything in this Universe. The accumulation, aggravation and pacification of *doṣa*s are time-dependent. The changes in the environment like heat and cold are also time-dependent. As per this theory the death is also time-dependent.

4. ***Yadṛcci*** means "spontaneous" or "by accident." This theory explains that all the substances are disappearing and appearing suddenly and start getting maturing suddenly like plants, animals, abscess, etc. Hence death is a sadder phenomena or/and spontaneous one.

5. ***Niyati*** means the fixed order of things or self-restraint or self-command. This theory explains that the actions done by a being result into things. For example, the intake of incompatible foods and practise of unwholesome activities cause dreadful diseases. Likewise death is also the result of unwholesome practises or *niyati*.

6. ***Pariṇāma*** means transformation. This theory explains that all "beings" and all actions of beings in the universe and also the changes in the universe are due to phenomenal transformation. So death is a transformation-phenomena.

   The contemporary life-sciences are not proposing any direct theories in relation to death. But the following theories may be considered:

   1. *Genetic causes*: These are the properties determined by genetic factors present in cells and causes progressive cellular damage which ultimately causes death. In these causes three different factors are present, namely limited cell replication, pre-determined programme of cell-replication and irreparable damage to genetic material. The limited cell-replication is due to built-in-genetic programme. That limits the doubling potential of cells. This ultimately causes death of cells. The predetermined programme of cell-replication is the pre-determined series of events in relation to cell-replication leading ultimately to maturation of cells and causing death. Irreparable damage to genetic material causes errors of DNA Replication and ultimately this causes the death.

   2. *Immunological causes*: Immune system always plays an important role in protection of body from biological agents. But the same may cause life-threatening situations which ultimately cause death, as for example the anaphylactic reaction to foreign protein (bacteria, virus, etc.) The endogenous self-antigens also sometime cause the same type of reactions which may take the person into death. With this background one can say that one may die due to immune reactions.

   3. *Nutritional causes*: No doubt nutrition is important to everybody. There are reported deaths from

different pockets of the world because of drought leading to scarcity of food and drinking water. Even in the conditions where surplus food production and supplies are present, deaths are reported due to vitamin deficiencies in countries where high standards of lifestyle are followed. Apart from this, the overnutrition or excess nutrition also causes death. For not only fat rich diet causes obesity arteriosclerosis and sudden death but also the high concentration of glucose can cause death by deranging the environment of tissues (cellular level). So one can infer that death may happen due to nutrition causes.

4. *Chemicals and drug causes*: Consumption of different chemicals and drugs has become high as because of changed lifestyles. These are very common and important causes for death. The chemicals and drugs can cause death in two ways: sudden death and slow death. Poisonous substances can cause death suddenly by producing sudden changes in the internal cosmos, whereas the noxious substances can cause death slowly altering the different mechanisms of body when used for long time. So death can happen due to the chemicals and drugs.

5. *Physical agents*: Physical agents like microbes, heat, radiant energy, atmospheric pressure and electric energy influence the beings. Both negative and positive extremes of the above agents along with the trauma can cause death as is known by everybody. Thus death can occur by physical agents.

6. *Psycho-neuro endocrinal causes*: Changes in the internal atmospheric/environment can produce death due to the alterations in the psycho-neuro-humoral axis. For example, sudden information of extraordinary emotions can result in death.

7. *Internal (metabolic) causes*: There are so many hundreds of metabolic reactions happening in the body at any given time. Because of these, high amounts of harmful products (free radicals) and non-harmful products are going to be released and also waste-products are produced. All these harmful products and waste-products will be removed through different mechanisms. Disturbances in these mechanisms can cause accumulation of these products and these further lead to cellular injury and further the cause of death.

There are example of false death or apparent death. This is a state in which a person looks or lives like dead. The functions of nervous system, circulatory system and respiratory systems may become very feeble or very minimum. The vital functions are not identified by conventional methods. The false death can be appreciated when the functions of the systems of that person "return" to normal after sometime with the help of resuscitation programme or even without it. This type of apparent death or false death is known among the yogic communities. It is also possible in certain circumstances like drowning situations. There are reports of persons having survived after several hours of drowning.

Āyurveda is the science of life which deals with preventive and curative aspects of health and disease respectively. To treat the patients, the doctor should know not only the different pathological states of diseases but also the death-indication symptoms. The understanding of death and its indicating symptoms are highly useful to a doctor, to inform the patient's relatives regarding the prognosis of the disease. It is also important in importing the necessary treatment in a given situation. *Āyurveda* advocates the treatment to be continued, till the time the *prāṇa* is present in the *kaṇṭha* (one of the *prāṇa sthānas*). And also, it is necessary to do the special (or) different types of treatment (procedure) in the critical state of life, i.e., approaching death. The understanding of death and its indicating symptoms must always be considered along these lines. There are a good amount of elaborative descriptions available in the *Āyurveda* relating to death indicating symptoms. These symptoms are called as *ariṣṭalakṣaṇās* in *Āyurveda*. These symptoms definitely occur in every patient before death. Once these symptoms are generated the patient is about to die.

The death indicating symptoms (*ariṣṭa lakṣaṛas*) can be divided into two types: *puruṣa sāṁśraya lakṣaṇas* which can be seen in patients and *puruṣa anāśraya lakṣaṇas* which can be seen not only in patients but also in the relatives, friends, environment, atmosphere, social aspects, etc.

1. ***Puruṣa Sāṁśraya lakṣaṇas*** can be seen or is present in the dying person. These are of three types: (a) *Lakṣaṇa nimittu lakṣaṇas*: These are present in every person from the time of birth, e.g., *hasta, pāda rekhās* (lines in the hands and feet), moles in different places which can be studied in *sāmudrika śāstra*, (b) *lakṣya nimitta lakṣaṇa*: They appear due to improper intake of *āhāra* (food), *vihāra* (behaviour in diseased persons), (c) *nimitta anurūpa lakṣaṇas*: They appear without any reason and definitely indicate death appearing in everybody before the actual death.

2. ***Puruṣa anāśraya***: These types of death indicating symptoms are of two types: (a) In relation to patient: sudden changes in the family situations (e.g., sudden bankruptcy of patient's family or accidents to family members), sudden changes in society and also unavoidable obstacles to the caller, who calls the doctor for treatment, etc., (b) In relation with treatment: not getting the proper or exact medicine or medicament, non-availability of equiment needed for treatment, etc.

This particular thought (concept and symptoms) is peculiar to *Āyurveda*. The *ariṣṭa lakṣaṇas* give the idea of forthcoming changes in the life-process. The life is nothing but the happenings in the energetical activities at different levels in micro-cosmos. This is accepted both in traditional thought and modern concept.

12

Death in Tibetan Science

L. Tenzin

No afflicted creatures imputed upon five aggregates could escape to a place where there are no deaths. Death is certain to every creature on this cyclic existence. Even the manifold methods of *mantra*-chanting and the power of modern skills can't refuge the uncertainty of death. Still then, the majority of the migratory (sentient beings) are not ready to come out with the analytic mental approach to the event of the so-called Death.

However, human beings are eventually far more superior and more brilliant than other migratory creatures in the field of principles of socialistic theories and more confirmed with the philosophies of the life. Because of this fact the modern human beings are highly equipped with the preplanned dynamic systems of philosophies in every aspect of life from the time immemorial, propounded by the great ancient sages or philosophers. Their noteworthy features of philosophical views are in their educational schemes of their times which are depicted in every systems of religious tenets. By the course of time, in our world it is proving increasingly necessary to bring oriental wisdom and occidental thinking into a synthesis on a higher plane of awareness to the material world. The occident has progressed technologically and materially to a tremendous degree such that the entire human societies are particularly influenced by the Occidentalism which has exerted a great influence on the material life of all the people. Human society becomes the slave to magnificent ideals of the advancement of nuclear power and such is the period where the entire modern society get empowered by the oriental development of chemical powers. Yet, for some mysterious reason the reality of death remains hidden from our immediate environments. Our response to the constantly pressing reality of death has changed with the trends of the passing century. Ours is the great cosmetic civilization, and nowhere is this quality of our age so obvious as our attitudes and habits regarding death and dying. We refuses to face the reality of death and divert all our money and energies to direct the lives and enhancements. For this, people are engrossed in money-making with their utmost effort and in this dimension, no matter how we try, nowhere do we attain absolute happiness rather we only encounter the power of death, which totally makes us shocked and we get perplexed during the clear light of death; the subtle mind that manifests at death following the experiences of the stages of dissolution of the elements and the gross minds of a person are two different things. Still then, one is obviously not ready to grasp the fact about the death and its consequences. For instance, how and when does death encounter with one, and what would be there after death. Here I attempt to give a glimpse of the basic causes of death related to the six innate elements of the human beings, who have taken birth in this world from mother's womb. The concept of the causes of death is being discused under the following headings:

Subtle Signs of Death — Experienced by Other Persons to Other Persons

The subject of death and dying has fascinated human beings from time immemorial, or we may say, ever since our intelligence developed to the point where we could realize the laws of impermanence.

Not only the human but also every existing creatures on this earth meets death. Human beings are the product of the temporary conjunction of five constantly changing orders of phenomena. Consciousness is the centralizing principle for all sensory information and thus the seat of discursive thought, underpinned by subconsciousness, which transmigrates from one existence to another when the elements, which constitute the body, disintegrate on death. Therefore, death is fundamentally nothing than total separation of one's clear and centralizing mind from ones body (composite of five elements). However, the union of oncepresent consciousness and body is conditioned by certain factors of the past and they cannot be separated like opposite poles of the hills.

In fact, in all its aspects from the gross to the subtle, one's present clear consciousness is dependent on the composite body of five elements of the present life.

The dependence of present consciousness on the physical body and the differences in the formation of nervous system and immunology, results in variation of perception from individual to individual. Likewise, it is obvious that experiences and indications of signs regarding the prediction of the impending death of the humans differ from one person to another.

For this, there are some person who can predict the exact death of the "other person by other person."

Now I will be dealing with how the Tibetan physicians can experience future prospects and predict the imminent death of a patient. This predicition and indication of a patient's death by the physician is not similar to that of falling mountains and houses that one's eyes hold at the very time of destruction.

It can be known and grasped gradually by judging the functional units of the five vital organs and six reservoirs and some other crucial organs of the patient. By going through all these observations, physicians can draw a point that how far the patient will sustain his/her life. Despite this, the physician makes a different preliminary test on the disease of the person from every angle and thereby he may gauge the patient's state of health and future prospects. He may even predict how and when will the deceased may encounter his impending death. Some inauspicious gross signs shown by the patient's disease, on the basis of which a doctor may gauge. The patient's state of health and his future prospects are as follows:

1. Total blockage of food intake due to the loss of appetite. Disturbances are caused because of the imbalance in diet due to the loss of appetite. Even if one takes enough nutritious food and drinks they show no sign of improvement in the bodily constituents. Rather there occurs a gradual depletion of the muscles so much so that the patient's skin on his skull appears to be like a thin covering.
2. When the channels of wind and blood are blocked and damaged by humorial imbalances they lead to a weaker frequency of pulsation of a body-part.
3. If the physicians make a correct diagnosis of the disease of heat-nature but whose antidote is ineffective owing to rise in secondary diseases like cold diseases and thereby due to the diminution of the digestive warmth, it would result in the formation of dropsy in our body. Similar is the result if the situation is vice-versa, i.e., even a correct diagnosis of cold-disease leads to a fully developed disease if its antidote is ineffective to the disease of heat nature.
4. If an inexpert physician, whose treatment is not appropriate, practises a preliminary treatment then the disease gets aggravated further which may lead to a general debility in bodily constituents of a patient.
5. The incubation period of the diseases has crossed the exact date.

6. The patient cannot respond to the therapeutic medicine due to the general debility in the bodily constituents.

The subtle pathological signs and indications of one's impending death can be prognosticated by the examination of the signs of life-span principles or the pulse of life essence (*bla-tsa*). Despite this, it can be done by reading the pulsation frequency of wind and blood in the circulatory channel, whose entire dispositions are predominantly windy. The nature of the pulse rate and the layout of the pulse of the entire disorderliness may differ from disease to disease. This can be exemplified as the flapping of a flag on the high steep mountains. For instance, though during the stage of the fever the pulse is initially fast, steep and aggressive in nature, if the initial frequency of the pulse while pressing the pulse changes into different rhymes, then the means of averting death of the patient is quite remote and one is expected to die shortly.

If the pulse of wind-disorder has rapid frequency then it implies that imminent death is approaching soon to the patient. If the phlegm-disorder has the elongated pulsation and sometimes shows no pulse channel, then some kind of inauspicious event is about to occur. These are a few of the signs, which portend death, perceived from the pulse of the ill-person.

Some other signs of sudden death regarding the pulse of patients are as follows:

If the pulse of the newly affected patient is poor, then it indicates that death may be on the way despite the fact that one has apparently superb bodily constituents. Being the victim of the disease for a long period, depletion of the bodily constituents will occur naturally, but now the frequency of the ailing man's pulse is strong and fast. This symptom warns of the impending death.

Death is also portended if certain different pulse rate enters into a initial pulse rate of the person under diagnosis. For instance, if a person cold in nature experiences the pulse of hot diseases or vice-versa, then it should be taken as a sign of impending death.

Besides these, pulse-prognostications, based on the constitution of pulses and the other pulse defects and pulsology, are also applied to indicate the following diseases resulting in the death of a patient:

1. The disease of lung inflammations,
2. Disease of meat,
3. Disorderliness caused by combining bile juice in stomach (digestive warmth system).
4. Disorderliness caused by combining phlegm in stomach (digestive warmth system).

It is to be noted that even if the pulse of a victim of the above-mentioned diseases shows no signs of such defects from his pulse channel, he is sure to face death soon.

Some imminent signs of one's impending death detected from the inner and outer pulse defect, caused by the agitation of bodily constituents and improper circulation of blood and wind in the channels of five vital organs and six crucial reservoirs are as follows:

If the pulsation frequency of heart is not channellizing in its own channel and also in the other organs and the darkening of tongue and bulging of eyes occur at the same time, then it should be taken as an indication that the patient will die after one day.

If the pulse of lungs are missing from its own channels, thereby among the organs, if nostril contraction and rising of inner hairs upwardly happen simultaneously then the patient will leave this world after two days. Likewise, if the pulse of the liver is not channellizing in its own channel and at the same time if the eyebrow becomes circular by holding one's eyes upward, then the patient will leave after three days, because of serious defects in the functional unit of liver.

It the pulse frequency of spleen is not channellizing in its own channel, then the deceased will die after five days, because of serious defect in the functional unit of the spleen.

Likewise, if the pulse of kidney is missing from its own channel, due to the failure of functional unit of kidney, and a defect in hearing power happen simultaneously, then the patient may leave this world after eight days.

Similar to this, if the pulse of life-essence does not move in between the tendons of the wrist, then the deceased will leave this world soon.

Prognostication of Impending Death by Urine Analysis

The law of *karma* is the constitution of all phenomena and all phenomena including the human beings exist in the momentary flux of cause and effect. One will certainly entertain his life at the best of his efforts until his kārmic merit lasted. At the very time of its exhaustion, the five primordial elements of our body will again contribute its role on the destruction of our body, thereby at a certain period by causing disturbances in the balance of our cardinal humour, bodily constituents and impurities, which once are primary building units of this very dying body. (At this very moment of destruction of our body, each of these elements is enemy of every other element and tries their best to defeat one another letting the body of ours frail.) Hence urine analysis may also prognosticate a fatal outcome for instance. Urine indicative of impending death through heat disorder is continuously blood-red which remains unchanged despite treatments.

Urine indicative of impending death through cold disorder is continuously light blue, without odour, vapour, suspension or bubbles.

Urine indicative of impending death through wind disorders is dark blue, its clear liquid and residue separating and forming patterns in the manner of cooked food. Despite all these, the signs of one's death through the bile disorders has clear liquid and impurities, which separate in the manner of rhubarb decoction. Urine suggestive of impending death through phlegm disorder resembles sour milk, while a specimen suggesting one's death through poison has clear liquid and residue which separate in the manner of black ink diluted with water.

Furthermore, the urine of patients afflicted by wind disorders has a fire-like suspensions of flowers and bile disorders. Urine has the colour of blood-red, while urine prognosticating death through blood disorders resembles vermilion adhering to the interior of its container.

Signs Related to Motiveless and Sudden Changes in the Behaviour

Though every human being believes and extends enough response to the constantly pressing reality of one's impending death and its cause, everyone is obvious with the fact that one will also leave this world by any means at any cost, no matter whatever the status one enjoys during the lifetime. Still one has the attitude and habits of neglecting this very inauspicious occasion and its consequences. Some perceives that death will encounter certainly, but this perception is a little far from its reality. One should spend enough time to analyse the realities about the causes and effects of this inauspicious day.

So a few more points relating to the prognostication of one's impending death are being given below:

The signs related to motiveless and sudden changes in the behaviour, in one's appearances or surrounding conditions indicate that death may be on the way despite the fact that one might apparently be in sound health. Thus, if one is displeased with the doctor, meditation or spiritual *guru* for no apparent reason or if intellectual and physical qualities or prosperity suddenly improves or deteriorates, these are held to be indications of his approaching death. The same applies to intakes of severe depression or imbecility or if changing attitudes to friends and enemies of long standing. He is not going to live long in this world whose complexion suddely becomes lackluster, whose *Torma* — offerings are not consumed by crows, whose body after ablutions dries out quickly around the heart, whose finger-joints do not crack when pulled, whose vigour deteriorates despite good nutrition, whose body is infected with lice and nits or so all on a sudden and their sudden disappearance too. Death is also portended by such changes in behaviours as when one experiences a dramatic rise or decline in desire or when a good tempered person becomes petulant, an energetic one lethargic and a generous one miserly or vice versa. If someone cannot cast a shadow on a sunny day, if a mirror or water do not reflect his image or if the image appears deformed or incomplete, lacking for example a head or hang two heads. Such persons will soon succumb to death.

In addition, death is sure for those people, if bleeding occurs from any of the nine bodily orifices without any secondary causes like weapon or poison. The signs of an imminent death concern either the dissolution of five primordial elements or the dysfunction of the five sensory organs. On the brink of death, the patient's nose begins to flare, accumulating dry mucus, while the tongue darkens, dries up, shortens and loses the ability to speak. The lower lip hangs down while the upper lip protrudes upward, the eyes become dull and the pupils dim, the breath becomes cold and spasmodic, the bodily heat disappears. These are a few of the signs of one's impending death experienced by oneself.

Signs Appearing in Dream whereby the Doctor may Gauge the Patient's State of Health and Future Prospects

In case of a diseased organism, inauspicious dreams, including those, which portend death, may be perceived when the channels of consciousness are blocked and damaged by *humorial* imbalances. Among the specific dreams, if the patient dreams of nakedly riding a buffalo, monkey, etc., this implies that the lasso of the lord of death ensnares him.

Similarly, if the patient dreams that plants grow from his body or if he has sensations of falling or of sleeping in the charnel ground or being encircled by spirits, ravens or villains, death is said to be at hand. If one dreams of being eaten or swallowed by fish and crocodile, death is sure for a dreamer. There are certain dreams which suggest that death will be caused by diseases of blood and bile, namely, when dreaming of drinking ale and dancing with deceased relatives, being dressed in red, or abducted by a laughing women, entering into mother's womb, scratching one's skin and shaving one's beard. Certainly these imply that death is not very far. Certain dreams forbode death that lead to specific diseases, such as consumption, tumours, leprosy and urinary problems. In addition, insanity, epilepsy and blindness may also portend death. Such dreams are inauspicious even when dreamed by one who is in good health because they indicate that the mind is in a potential state of humorial imbalance. It is important to remember, however, that the consequences of a negative dream may be diminished if various purificatory practises, such as burnt-offerings are made and meditation is subsequently performed.

Signs of one's Impending Death Experienced by Deceased Himself

If five vital organs and six crucial reservoirs are afflicted by any serious diseases or caused by the weapons and poisons, one is sure to suffer from unbearable pains around the affected areas of the vital organs. The distorted and non-discerning mind of the deceased will fully lose hope for his recovery from the disease and his wrongly conceived perception about the nature of the death will vanish during this very clear light of his death. Despite this, if there are certain changes in the behaviours of the doctors and the surrounding people; then the dying himself confirms that he will be no longer the member of this world. This directly implies that the dying person will die soon.

Other signs of an imminent death are the dissolution of the five primordial elements or the dysfunction of the five sensory organs. The elements are absorbed successively into each other by leaving two impressions in the mind of the patient. That is by leaving two significant signs, external and internal, of one's impending death:

1. The external and internal signs of one's impending death upon the sinking of the earth element in the water elements are:

   Our body begins to lose all its strength. All energy gets drained of and we become unable to get up and stay upright or hold anything. We can no longer support our head. We feel as though we are falling, sinking or being crushed by a great weight. We may even ask our relatives to pull us up. Our cheeks sink, and dark stains appear on our teeth. As the aggregate of form is dissolving, we become frail and weak. Our mind is agitated and delirious and finally sinks into drowsiness. The internal secret sign that appears in the mind is a vision of a shimmering mirage and appearances of bluish vision in one's mind.

2. The imminent external and internal signs of one's impending death, while sinking of water element in fire are:

   We begin to lose control of our bodily fluid. Our nose begins to run, and we dribble.

   Our nostril begins to flare, accumulating dry mucus. While the tongue dries up, it gets shortened and loses the ability to speak. Our lips are drawn and become bloodless and our mouth and throat become sticky and clogged. The nostrils cave in and we feel thirsty. We tremble and twitch. The smell of death begins to hang over us. As the aggregates of feeling are dissolving, bodily sensations dwindle, alternating between pain and pleasure, heat and cold.

The internal secret is a vision of haze with swirling wisps of smoke, or sensing a bluish smoke-filled house.

3. The external and internal signs of one's impending death upon the sinking of fire element in air elements are:

   Our mouth and nose dry up completely. All the warmth of our body begins to seep away, usually from the feet and hands towards the heart. We lose the odour and taste-power and breathing problem occurs. The aggregate perception is dissolving and our mind swings alternately between clarity and confusion. So the internal secret-sign is of shimmering red sparks, dancing above an open fire, like fireflies.

4. Similar to this, the external and internal signs of one's impending death while sinking of air elements in the consciousness:

   It becomes harder and harder to breathe. The air seems to be escaping through our throat. We begin to rasp and pant. Our in-breaths become short and laboured. Our breaths become longer and continue to be more shallow and outer breaths become longer. At this point blood gathers and enters the "channel of life" in the centre of our heart and three drops of blood collected one after another causing three long final breaths. Then suddenly our breathing ceases. What is happening is that if the air element is dissolving into consciousness, the winds have all united in the "life supporting wind." This is described as a vision of a flaming torch or lamp, with a red glow. All the vital signs are gone and this is the point where in a modern clinical situation we would be certified as dead.

The inner dissolution, where gross and subtle levels of consciousness are to be encountered, for instance, during the sinking of consciousness into any elements, the consciousness of the dying person has to encounter with the following four phases.

1. Appearance (*nangwa*)
2. Increase (*chepa*)
3. Full attainment (*chepa thoppa*)
4. "the mind of clear light of death" (*thamche tongpa ma yee vorsel*).

During the sinking of air element into the consciousness, initially we experience a reddish sparkling fire of butter lamp and after that there is an experience of "whiteness" like a pure sky. Struck by moonlight and inner sign are that our awareness becomes extremely clear and all the thought states end. This phase is known as "Appearance."

During the sinking of "visualizing power into imminent gaining" we experience of "redness" like a sun shining in a pure sky.

During the sinking of "Appearance" into the "Increase" phase we experience "redness" like a sun shining in a pure sky and the inner sign is that, there arises a great experience of bliss, as all the thought-states resulting cease to function. This phase is known as "Increase" phase.

During the sinking of "increase" stage into the "full attainment" one experiences blackness like an empty sky, shrouded in utter darkness. The inner sign is an experience of a state of mind free of thoughts and consciousness is enclosed between the red and white essences. Every thought-states result from ignorance and delusions are brought to an end.

This is known as "full attainment." While sinking of "full attainment" into the "mind of clear lights of death," we become slightly conscious again, the ground luminosity dawns, like an immaculate, sky free of cloud, fog or mist. This is called "the mind of clear light of death."

After this our very consciousness vanishes away and will go through the state (*bardo*) for future rebirth.

In a nutshell, as far as the five sensory organs born out of the five primordial elements are concerned, the first that ceases to function is sight, then comes the ability to hear, followed by the sense of smell, taste and finally touch. Consequent on this tactile dysfunction, life itself wanes and all sensory functions dissolve into the "life sustaining breath," which itself vanishes into the consciousness, destined for future re-birth. Thus during conception when the body is initially formed, the five primordial elements contribute to the embryonic developments. In the intermediate period of physical growth, they co-exist peacefully and in the final period of body's dissolution they agitate each other, causing the body's own destruction.

So ours is the great cosmetic civilization and nowhere is this quality of our age so obvious as our attitude and habits regarding the death and dying. Thus, we consider this topic as a child's play.

13

Death in Prehispanic Mexico

Yolotl González Torres

It is said that in Mexico people are not afraid of death and that they laugh at it. Although this is not quite true, there are many representations of death, specially some caricatures in the form of skeletons criticizing notorious social and political characters which were published at the end of the nineteenth century, which were quite hilarious. This custom has become a sort of tradition and every year around the celebration of the dead in November, the newspapers publish caricatures portraying public people transformed into skeletons accompanied by some verses in the form of funny epitaphs.

Even today skeletons for the celebration of the day of the dead are not only used as ornamental motives but skulls made of sugar or chocolate with the name of a person drawn in the front are given as present to friends or put on the altar of the dead along with other offerings. People from other countries find this custom rather macabre, but Mexicans see it very natural.

There is still the custom, which is disappearing with the introduction of the North American Halloween, to erect, on the 1st and 2nd of November, on the Day of the Death, an altar with offerings for the deceased relatives. These offerings include yellow flowers (marigolds), candles, copal and incense made of the resin of a tree and special food and drink and sugar skulls. It is believed that the souls of dead people come to visit their relatives on this day to enjoy all the items which are placed on the altar. If no offerings are given to them, they become very sad and angry and may even hurt their careless relatives.

Many people go to the cemetery where they clean and arrange the tombs and put offerings on it, including the eatables. After some ceremony they think, the dead have taken their share of the food. This is followed by a feast of the food and drink. Most of the times, they get drunk and make a feast during the celebrations for their dead.

The date of celebration of the dead has changed after the conquest. It is now on the 1st and the 2nd of November, following the Catholic calendar but the ritual and the feeling are still prehispanic. The Catholics too, have rituals to remember their dead and to help them reach salvation where reached the souls of people who led a pious life on earth. According to the canons of the Catholic church, the souls of people who led a pious life live in the heavens, and they are in a constant state of bliss among the other celestial beings, like the Virgin Mary and the Saints. The last two are believed to help the souls of the deceased who were in purgatory, an intermediate place of purification. After a time of punishment in the purgatory, the souls could go to the heavens, but the great sinners went to the hell, a terrible place of eternal damnation. The concept of hell which did not exist in the prehispanic cosmovision was one of the images with which the Catholic priests frightened the Indians if they did not convert to Catholicism.

In spite of conversion, voluntary or forced, the Indians kept many of their beliefs and practices, at different levels of syncretism with a popular type of Catholicism.

For the ancient Mexicans, death and all its symbols were a part of common life. An ominous remainder of the futility of life and, at the same time, of the might of the Mexican Empire were the *tzompantli* "wall of heads," located at the centre of Tenochtitlan, their capital city. It was an enormous rack where hundreds of trophy-heads of sacrificial victims were placed. Perhaps death played such an important part in ancient Mexico because it was believed that men had been created to serve and to nourish the gods, especially the Sun. In a way, the Mexicans thought about themselves as a predestined people who had the task to nourish the Sun with the hearts and blood of sacrifices, in order that he would continue to shine, which meant the continuity of life for the whole cosmos.

This conception could be extended to the gods of earth, water and nourishment, who were offered the hearts and blood of children, women and men, so that they could respond by giving life and nourishment to the people.

In spite of the importance of death among the Mexicans we don't know with certitude many things about their actual beliefs of the destiny of the soul, whether it totally disappear after sometime or whether it remain in the land of the death or whether some souls of them would return in another form of life.

The Mexicans believed as many other people in the world, that there was a material body and some "animical entities," souls or energies, which could leave the body temporally during sleep, trances or certain illness or definitely during death. According to Lopez Austin (1980), they believed that there were three "animical entities": two of them were a sort of hot and cold life-forces which permeated the universe and were related to the sun and fire on the one hand and to the moon, water and earth on the other. These two life-forces had to be in equilibrium in order to be healthy and well. The hot life-force or *tona* was the one which was given to the sun as a sort of fuel, when a person was sacrificed and a lack of it could cause illness or even death. This energy was also linked to a person's destiny working in a similar manner as astrology does and there were also specialists who dealt with illness caused by *tona* or divined through a special count (González 1976).

The third animical entity is the one which could be equated to a soul or a ghost, and it was this the one which gets placed in the foetus after conception by the goddess Citlalinicue, "the one with a skirt of stars" who lived in the heavens. This soul, was also the one who travelled during dreams and left the body after death to rest in its particular abode.

There were different rituals when a man or a woman died, which varied according to the way they had died and to their social position. A little stone, a simple pebble or a jade stone regardless of whether he was a simple peasant or a noble person is generally placed in the mouth of the corpse as heart. The body is washed, a tuft of hair from the top of head which is believed to keep some of the *tona,* was cut and kept by the relatives. The body is placed in a sitting position and enveloped in sheets of dark paper. A dog of red hair was killed to accompany the body and if the dead man was a king he was dressed with ornaments of his patron-god, and some of the concubines, officers and slaves were killed to accompany him. Then the body was burnt and the remains were sprinkled with water and kept in a ceramic jar along with the pebble and the tuft of hair from the top of the head. The remains of common people were buried in the family houses and in the case of the kings or important people, in the temples of the principal gods (González 1975).

The remains were put in a box painted inside with figures of the devil and to shroud or cover the face they put a mask on it. And on top of this they make a wooden figure which is the image of the deceased-master. Before it, they pay homage. They visit later the deceased's wives and his relatives. This ceremony is called Quitonaltia (Motolinia 1967).

During the following four days after the death of the person, daily or even twice a day, offerings were taken to that place where the body had been burnt and where the remains were kept in the ceramic jar. At the fourth day when it was believed that the deceased's journey to the final abode was over a bigger ceremony was performed and if the deceased was a rich or a noble person, new human offerings were made.

Among the discoveries of the many archaeological excavations in 1994 two archaeologists discovered at a place called "The eagle house," very near the remains of the Great temple of Tenochtitlan, the burial of an important warrior, which confirmed what the written sources say about the funerary customs.

The burial was at the feet of the stairs and there they found three ceramic vessels belonging to different epochs. Inside was the charred bones of a man — the same man — along with rich offerings including the burnt-bones of a dog, a jaguar, a kin eagle and a hawk plus different objects made of obsidian, flint, basalt, greenstone, turquoise, gold, copper, bronze, pirita, conch, copal, cotton, pieces of textile, etc. (Roman *et al.*, 1999)

It was believed that after death the soul of the deceased had to go through a perilous journey which included passing through two huge rocks which were clashing against each other, and then through another place, where a big snake was lying. The soul also has to go through the place of a green lizard, and then through eight deserts and eight hills and through a wind of obsidian. They said that to help the soul pass through such a strong and cold wind the relatives burnt all the belongings of the dead and all the offerings. If it had been a warrior they burnt all his arms and all the spoils he had taken in war and if it was a woman all her dresses and tools for weaving.

At last the soul arrived to the shores of the river Chiconahuapan where the red haired dog who had been killed and burnt with his body was waiting to carry him across the river. On the other side of it they meet with Mictlantecuhtli, the lord of death and his wife, who offer to him all the presents which had been given to him by his relatives.

The warriors who had died in a battle, or the *pochteca* — businessmen — who had died during their business trips, their funerary rituals were carried out without their bodies and instead their effigy was made of canes and paper. For eighty days, after the death, the deceased's wife and near relatives were not allowed to comb their hair or wash themselves.

The people who died through water or the women who died in their first parturition were buried instead of burnt. The bodies of the latter, especially the forearms were believed to possess magical properties which would give power to the warriors and witches and so the husbands and relatives of the dead women had to keep guard on her tomb, so that their bodies are not stolen.

After twenty, forty, sixty and eighty days of death especially after the ceremonies had been performed and again, if the dead man had been of a high social position, new human victims were offered. Afterwards every year new offerings were made to the remains kept in the ceramic vessel.

The place where the soul went varied according to the way the person died, and not according to his or her behaviour in life: men who died in battle or through sacrifice went to *Tonatiuixco*, "the place of the sun," a sort of paradise, which was located in the East, while the women who died during their first childbirth went to the western land of the sun. Both, warriors and women accompanied the sun on his way through the sky. The warriors, holding their arches, arrows and shields picked up the sun when it first appeared in the eastern sky and left it at the zenith, where it was picked up by the women who left it on the West where it went to the underworld, to the land of the dead. After four years of death the souls of the warriors become birds of beautiful colours or butterflies who could come to drink flower nectar on the earth.

Also to the land of the sun, went the pochteca if they died while on their business journey. The babies who were still breast-feeding went to a place called *chichihuacuauhco*, "the tree of breasts" where there was a big tree full of breasts, where the souls of the babies could suck at and be nourished, and where they would wait to be reborn. Their bodies were buried in the granaries.

The people who died through a disease related to water, either drowned, hit by a thunderbolt, or by hydropsy or other diseases which they believed were related to water, went to *Tlalocan*, the paradise of Tlaloc, the god of water, which in some ways, was an enjoyable place full of gardens and water, of perpetual abundance of maize, pumpkins, green peppers, tomatoes, beans and flowers. While the people who died of old age or of natural diseases went to Mictlan, the land of the dead, ruled by Mictlantecuhtli, the Lord of death and his wife Mictecacihuatl, the lady of death.

This land of the dead which was located in the north and is described with all sorts of gloomy images, including one which says that there was no way out. The souls of people who stayed there lead a similar life to the one they had while they were alive. So the kings and people of the nobility had concubines and servants, whom as we said were killed to accompany the dead king or master. But also some of our sources say that after four years, the souls who went to Mictlan completely disappeared.

López Austin thinks that:

> Dead persons were forced to make important tasks in or from the other world where they had been located for instance, to lead the rain, to make the plants grow, to honour the sun on his way to cause or cure some types of illness, etc. For him, the fulfilment of a cosmic function was more important than a prize or a punishment. There were no paradises. They went to work in tasks that lasted for four years. This is an opinion which I mention but I don't think there are enough evidences to support it.

It was also said that dead kings were deified. According to Sahagún (1968):

> About him they used to say that he was Teotl (god), which means that he was dead, to be spirit or god; and the ancient ones believed . . . that when the lords died they became gods. We have further evidences that some of their main gods like Quetzalcoatl, Huitzilopochtli and Mixcoatl seem to have been important men who lived in former times and were deified and some of their relics were kept and became the most important objects of worship kept in a "sacred bundle" called the *tlaquimilolli*. Other human beings who were deified were the women who died in childbirth. When a midwife realized that in spite of her efforts to save the life of a young woman who had been in labour died, she is deified. And so the ones who die of childbirth, the so-called *mocihuaquetzque*, after they die, they say they become goddesses, and so when one of them dies, then the midwife prepares dresses and adorns her as a goddess before she is buried. The midwife addresses her thus: "You have earned with your death, eternal, joyful and enjoyable life, with the goddesses which are called *cihuapipiltin*, celestial goddesses. Therefore go now, my very dear beloved daughter, little by little go with them and be one of them. . . ."

These goddesses who were in a way evil spirits, they would come on certain days of the year to harass people, especially women and children, as a revenge for not having been able to have a child of their own and become mothers. They would bring diseases to children. So they had to be propitiated. They were represented as women dressed in white, most of the times with the face of a skeleton.

As mentioned before, most of the sources tell us that after these four years in the land of the dead the soul totally disappears. So the poem says:

> Perhaps a second time we have to live?
> Your heart knows it
> Just once we have come to live.

But there is a hint that children who died very young or the kings, warriors or the women who died in their first parturition could reincarnate as birds or insects or even as gods. As, a poem says:

> *In four years, in the other world there is a resurgence; people are not fixed in the place of the fleshless, in the house of quetzal feathers; there is a transformation of what belongs to the one who makes people reborn.*
>
> — Leo'n Portilla 1959

There are many interpretations by scholars of the beliefs of the destiny of the souls of the dead ancient Mexicans. Nicholson (1967) presents an interesting but rather fantastic and romantic interpretation:

> Tillan Tlapallen, "the land of the black and red,"is another place where the souls of the dead people went. Black and red in conjunction signify wisdom. This was the paradise of the initiates who had found a practical application for the teaching of the god-king Quetzalcoatl. It was the land of the fleshless, the place where people went who had learned to live outside their physical bodies or it would be better to say, unattached to them; a place celebrated in many ancient poems and greatly to be desired.
>
> Farther beyond was Tonatiuhuican, land of Tonatiuh, house of the sun, often misrepresented as a military-political abode of warriors; but this is only because the Nahua "holy war" has been wrongly interpreted as an earthly war against earthly enemies. The third paradise was probably reserved for those who achieved full illumination in the quest for deserved and eternal happiness. So there is a series of three paradises, each more prefect than the one below and to be attained only by ever more intense spiritualistic pursuits and sacrifices of the gross physical world. Men whose desires were for good food and gaiety would go to the land of water and mist and then return to earth. Those who had acquired some kind of immortality, apart from the perishable body would aspire to the land of the fleshless. And those who achieved still higher perfection might become worthy of living in the house of the sun. One's fate might of course be bad, causing one to go after death to the inferno called Mictlan, a dark place ruled over by the god, Mictlantecuhtli and his consort Mictlancihuatl. This place was at the centre of the earth, and much less desirable than the cloudlands of the warrior.

Nevertheless souls there did not suffer. They merely endured a rather colourless existence, perhaps the worst fate of all.

References

León Portilla, Miguel 1959, *La Filosofia náhuatl estudiada en sus fuentes*, UNAM, Mexico.

López Austin, Alfredo, 1989, *Cuerpo humanoe ldeologia*, UNAM, Mexico.

———, 1999, "Misterios de la vida y la muerte," *Arqueologia Mexicana*, vol. VII, num 40, pp. 4-10, Mexico.

Motolinia, Fray Toribio, 1967, *Apologética Historia Sumaria*, UNAM, Mexico.

Nicholson, Irene, 1967, *Mexican and Central American Mythology*, Paul Hamlyn (ed.), London.

Roman, Ballereza, Juan Alberto and López Lujan, Leonardo, 1999, "El funeral de un dignatorio mexica," *Arqueologia Mexicana*, vol. VII, no. 40, pp. 36-45, Mexico.

Sahagún, Fray Bernardino, 1968, *Historia General de las cosas de la Nueva Espana*, ed. Porrua, Mexico.

Yolotl, González, Torres, 1975, "El culto a los muertos entre los mexica," *Boletin INAH*, Mexico, no. 14, pp. 37-44.

———, 1976, "El concepto de tona en el Mexico Antiguo," *Boletin, INAH*, Mexico, INAH, no. 19, pp. 13-16.

14

Death in Santal Thought

Onkar Prasad

DEATH is the most mysterious of all episodes in man's life. The Santals, a tribal community, do have their own idea about death. In their mythology, *Thakur Jiu* (Sun god), the creator of life on the earth, is said to be responsible for the origin of death. In ancient times, the death came as a punishment to human beings who broke the moral order of the community. As described in the *Baha* myth, when the descendants of *pilcu haram* and *pilcu budhi*, the primordial couple, became sinful and selfish to the extent that they even did not recognize each other, *Thakur Jiu* thought of destroying them. So he started raining fire. All, except the two, i.e., *pilcu haram* and *pilcu budhi*, who had hid themselves in a cave of Logo mountains, were destroyed. Thereupon *Thakur Jiu*, at the request of *maran buru* (great mountain) — one of the presiding deities of the tribe — rained water to cool down the earth, and later life on the earth sprang up again.

According to the Santals the death is nothing but the "flying away of soul" from the human body (*jivi udau kana*). As a result, two basic physical elements — earth and air — that constitute the human body with their respective components, i.e., the earthy body mixes with the earth (*hasa hormo hasare mitaua*), and the life merges with air (*hoy jijiban hoyare mitaua*). This perception regarding death affirms that the Santals believe in the existence of "soul" different from that of the human body. They also believe that after death the "soul" goes to live in a world different from that of the present one. These two beliefs have influenced the Santals at every stage of life, making them dependent on the supernatural world as reflected in their ritual practices associated with death.

The Santals believe that their existence on the earth is trouble-free only because of the benevolence of some supernatural powers. Therefore, they placate those powers on various ceremonial occasions and establish alliance with them. It is through them that they control the malevolent spirits responsible for the death of an individual. The Santals also attribute death to the impersonal powers and witchcraft. Death, in fact, is believed to be caused by the malignant agencies and the defeat of the benevolent spirits. Hence when a Santal dies, the family, the lineage and the village of the deceased are declared polluted and bereft of the favour of the "guardian spirits." To return to the normal state of affairs, the dead, who still remains a member of the family and not yet reached the country of the dead ancestors, has to be cremated and the purificatory rites have to be observed. Therefore, soon after the death, the dead body is taken out for cremation. It is laid out in a cot and smeared with oil and turmeric. Hands and the feet of the dead are washed with water and some water is also dropped in his mouth. Thereupon, the dead body is wrapped in a new white cloth. A number of articles are carried to the cremation ground such as a winnowing fan, a leaf plate, a spade, an axe, paddy and some burnt seeds of cotton, some turmeric paste, a small earthen pot, some powder of sun-dried rice, one fowl, a bundle of straw from the deceased's house and the end part of a rope of straw is lighted inside the house. Some articles like a battle axe, bow and arrow, brass cup, flute or drum, stick and some coins are piled on the cot with a belief that these would be required by the dead in the other world (*hanapuri*) to which he would be journeying. If the dead is a girl or a woman, her bangles, earrings and other ornaments are given as presents and piled on the bier. Thereupon, four men carry the corpse out into the street and pause at the junction of the road, where an *ojhā* exorcises the dead. From there, the corpse is brought to the cremation ground. The funeral pyre facing north-south is built there. The four persons now lift the cot and circumambulate the pyre three times. They place the cot on the pyre. All the gifts, as also the cot, are removed and the corpse is placed on the pyre. A fowl is pinned at the east of the pyre. Fire is now kindled from the lighted rope and is touched to the mouth by the chief mourner who is generally either the eldest or the youngest son. After that the pyre is set on fire requesting the dead body to burn itself out quickly when the pyre is set ablaze. The chief mourner and the villagers squat at a distance. There, a barber shaves their skull. After the dead body has been burnt completely the pyre is extinguished by pouring down water on it. Then chief mourner collects flowers of bones (*janba baha*), which consists of three pieces of bones — two from the skull and one from the collar. The "flowers" of bones are placed in a small earthen vessel. The vessel is covered with a lid having a crevice in its middle for the dead to breathe. It is believed that it is here that the dead man takes rest and his soul for the time being is contained in it. Later, when the pyre is completely extinct, the chief mourner moves to a distance along the river to take bath. When all have finished their bath, the chief mourner places the "flowers" of bones in three leaf plates; he puts a little bit of earth, and a tooth twig on each plate and finally lets them to float in the river towards the west. Thus, with the performance of this ritual the dead becomes an ancestor (*hapram*). Thereafter, all those who had gone to cremate the dead return to the village where some resin is burnt for them to inhale and to purify. Then, they return to their respective homes. Later, in the evening, the village elders visit the deceased's house to console the bereaved members of the family.

Purificatory Rites

This includes the performance of *Tel Nahan* and *Bhandan* rituals. *Tel Nahan* rite is observed either on the fifth or on the ninth day. All persons belonging to the same clan and the villagers gather in the house of the bereaved family. A barber shaves their skull. They all smear their bodies with oil to take a purificatory bath. Now, a ceremony follows. Three tooth sticks, each one of four fingers in length, oil cakes and some soapy earth are arranged on three *sal* leaves. These are offered to the *Maran Buru* (one of the presiding deities of the tribe), the deceased and the ancestors. While making the offering, *Maran Buru* is requested to admit the departed soul after purifying it with all these materials. Thereupon all the persons present there take a purificatory bath. They are provided rice-beer to drink. At night fowls are sacrificed and the members of the household worship *Maran Buru* as also the deceased. The death rituals conclude with a feast and drink. The deceased is also offered meal in a basket that is hung from a rafter of the house. The following morning the basket is observed closely to see as to whether the meal has been eaten by the spirit of the dead. The observance of *Tel Nahan* ceremony makes the village pollution-free, but the house remains polluted until the *Bhandan* ceremony is observed.

On the day fixed for *Bhandan*, all kinsmen come with a potful of rice-beer and a fowl or a pig. A pig and some fowls are also bought by the family of the deceased for sacrifice. The village chief and other elder members of the village also attend the ceremony. The village barber serves the male members. Thereupon both men and women take bath in a nearby pond or river. On return two persons impersonate *Maran Buru* and the deceased. Both make guttural sounds and shake their heads. One of the relatives call on the name of the deceased and the dead in turn demands water from all inmates and relatives and also from the villagers. Rice-beer is also offered to both. The *Jog Majhi* (assistant priest) now erects a *sal* branch in the courtyard of the dead where the chief mourner sacrifices a fowl by clubbing it on its head. A goat is sacrificed for the spirit of the dead person invoking the deceased to protect the living relatives from any danger. Libation of rice-beer is also made. This follows drinking of rice-beer by all those present. At night the chief mourner offers some food to the departed soul invoking to accept and purify the house completely. In this way all the rites associated with death come to an end.

However, if a Santal dies of an infectious disease, like cholera, small pox, etc., the body of the deceased is buried in a grave, dug in the direction of north to south, with two slots in each of its walls for the dead to breathe. Prior to burying the dead body a cloth is laid in the grave and the body is placed on it. Thereupon, a fowl is pinned inside the grave to accompany the soul to the other world. The grave is filled with earth. The boulders are also placed over the mound and a hedge of thorns is built to protect the body from animals. Finally, the site is purified with cowdung and water and the mourners leave the place for their homes. If a pregnant woman dies, her foetus is removed from the belly and buried but the woman is cremated. If a child dies before it learns to talk, it is buried but no ceremony is observed further.

Ritual practices associated with the death reveal that the Santals believe in continuity of life even after death. This is also manifested through initiation ceremony that speaks of the Santal attitude towards death. During initiation ceremony, for example, a Santal male child is cicatrized with three marks (*sika*) on his fore-arm, each symbolizing life (*jion*), death (*moron*) and the life (*jion*) again respectively. The Santals consider death as inauspicious and don't want to end up with death. Therefore, they hit upon an odd number of *sika* marks which will ensure life after death. The *sika* is also shown to the guardian of the other world after reaching the world of dead. If a Santal male is unable to show it, a giant worm resembling the size of the *Tumdak* (a cylindrical drum) would sit on his lap in the other world and torment him till he has been eaten up completely. A similar practice is followed in case of a female child. The female child, unlike the male child, is tattooed (*khoda*) before marriage on the left arm, shoulder and breast, and after marriage on the right arm, shoulder and breast. If she is unable to show the scars to the God of death, he would consider her impure and send her directly to the underworld. Whatsoever it may be, once the spirit of the dead has been sent to the other world it has to take birth again. That of course depends upon the nature of the deeds the individual has done during lifetime. An individual who has committed wrongs would be born as beasts or birds, and in case he has done good deeds he would be born again as a man. However, if a person has met an unnatural death or in the case of a woman dying in pregnancy or childbirth, full spiritual status cannot be achieved. They turn to the world of ghosts, and are believed to continue hovering around the world as *bhūta*s or *churin*s.

Conclusion

In a nutshell, it may be said, that the Santals think of the supernatural power as the origin of death. Death came as a curse to human beings and hence inauspicious. Further, the Santals believe in the continuity of life even after death. This has led them to observe funerary and purificatory rites for the smooth journey of the departed soul to the abode of ancestors as also for the release of the living survivors from the death-pollution. But persons having unnatural death are deprived of journeying to the abode of their ancestors, because of their not attaining the full spiritual status. The Santals also believe in rebirth. Beliefs in continuity of life after death and rebirth regulate the ways of life of the Santals in this world.

References

Archer, W.G., 1974, *The Hill of Flutes: Life, Love and Poetry in Tribal India*, New Delhi, S. Chand & Co.

Dupre, Wilhelm, 1975, *Religion in Primitive Cultures: A Study in Ethnophilosophy*, Mouton.

Mukherjee, C.L., 1962, *The Santals*, Calcutta: A. Mukherjee & Co.

Troisi, J., 1979, *Tribal Religion: Religious Beliefs and Practices Among the Santhals*, New Delhi, Manohar Publications.

15

Death Among The Saoras

M. Suryanarayana

SAORAS are one of the important primitive tribal groups in Andhra Pradesh with a population of 82,102 (1991). They speak a language known as Saora and it belongs to the Kolarian family. The survey is done in three different regions, i.e., Seetampeta (more isolated), Bhadragiri (less isolated) and Mandasa (more exposed) in Vijayanagaram and Śrīkākulam districts of Andhra Pradesh. In the present paper, the Saora concept of death and rituals associated to it have been discussed. Fieldwork on Saoras was undertaken for a period of time in different phases from 1965 to 1992.

Saora Concept of Death

The Saoras do not seem to have been in any way influenced by the Āryan conception of *svarga* or *devaloka*. They have their own conception of immortality of the body, with life which once existed, and the eternal immortality of the soul after death, and an eternal abode of the fathers. Labanamar is an interesting word in the Saora language. It means an immortal person. The first part of the compound *laban* literally means slough. But the Saoras generally believe that man once possessed the power of sloughing the skin and living young for ever. They regard the snakes and the monkeys to be naturally immortal, and death in their case must be due to actual killing. Hence the belief among the Saoras, *jadanalaba labaametel*, meaning, 'may you have the sloughing' — the sloughing of the snake ! 'may you live long.' There is also the saying *Anlen jadan pa? Alaba labanaba ode arsibaon karubaon deai*? Are we snakes to have the power of sloughing? Or are we the offspring of the monkey or of the baboon to live long and for ever?

The Saoras believe that the animals like the snakes have retained the power of sloughing; monkeys and baboons live for ever unless they are killed. They seem to argue that a person does not die unless he is actually killed. Some Saoras realize the rationalistic cause of death, but generally the ordinary Saora mind disregards or not satisfied with the rationalistic explanation given to account for the death of a particular person. In their loud lamentations, the nearest relatives like the mother of the deceased cry out: "What has become of you? What spirit has devoured you? Who has bewitched you? To whose malice have you become a victim?" etc.

Death is generally attributed by the Saoras to the malice of some malignant spirits or of a witch or wizard. The spirit kills the man by subjecting him to a disease which is frequently named after an evil spirit causing it. Even a fall from the tree is attributed to the influence of an evil spirit. The witch or wizard brings about the death of the person whom he or she desires to kill through the agency of a wicked spirit over which he or she has gained perfect control by acquisition of witchcraft.

According to the belief of the Saroas every person has two souls: (1) *rup rup puradan*, (2) *sanna puradan*. *Purada* seems to have come from Sanskrit *prāṇa*. *Rup rup* probably refers to the heart beat. The heart is said to be its seat. The *purada* is said to permeate the whole body, the excreta, the objects in contact with the body, the shadow of the body and even the object on which the shadow falls. Hence any object belonging to a person and charged with the substance of the *rup rup purada* can be used for magico-religious purposes. At the same time, according to the belief of the Saoras, this *purada* seems to be a separate entity having an existence independent of the body. It is invisible, personal, transmigrant and immortal. It can leave the body at will and freely wander and return to the body of the person to which it belongs. The Saoras account for dreams by saying that this *purada* undertakes its dream-land adventure while the body is asleep. Hence, dreams of the dead have produced in the Saora mind a strong conviction that this *purada* of the deceased is immortal.

Sanna purada normally is believed to leave the body temporarily during night. Hence a person after sunset is considered as half-dead. Accordingly, Saoras avoid sex during nights, as it implies having sex with half-dead. It is also a taboo to have sex in the house as they believe that ancestral spirits rest in the spot dedicated, and hung over the roof in the house. To have sex in their vicinity is considered bad. They have sex in their respective fields, in the bushes during the day time.

The absence of this *purada* for a long time is considered dangerous, because it may be captured by a sorcerer, and prevented from returning to the body. This *purada* cannot stay in the body for a long time without receiving its energy from the first *purada*. Death becomes the final departure of the first *purada*. After leaving the body finally, the *rup rup purada* is no longer known by that name; it becomes a *kulba* or ghost. The *kulba* is supposed to be fond of and attached to the house and to reside on a tree in the vicinity of the house in the case of a premature death of a person. Such a *kulba* is believed to be eager to be born again in the family to which it belongs. It sometimes appears to a surviving member of the family in his dream, and informs him that it is going to be born again in the house. The expectant mother in the house, if there be one, is then supposed to give birth to a child which is charged with the *rup rup purada*, relating the *kulba*. The child born in these circumstances is named after the person whose *kulba* appeared in the dream. A grandson is not named after the grandfather if he is born while the latter is still alive, because the *rup rup purada*s of the two are evidently different.

The *kulba* of a person that dies in his ripe old age is supposed to be devoid of any attachment and is, therefore, eager to go to the world of the ancestors (*kinorai-desa*) or the abode of the *jojongi* and *yoyongi*.

But the *kulba* cannot go to the eternal abode of the ancestors till the funeral rites have been completely performed. The same belief prevails among the Āryanized Hindus; the *preta* of the Āryans corresponding to the Saora *kulba* goes to the *pitṛloka* after the funeral ceremony has been completed. The final funeral ceremony among the Saoras is called *guar* which literally means "planting (memorial) stones." Each of the dead is represented by a stone slab, large or small, according to the rank and the age of the dead person. For the sake of convenience and economy, the *guar* is performed in each lineage once in two years or more so that all the bereaved families may jointly do it. The stones are planted in a fixed spot outside the village with all the pomp and ceremony. Ten to thirty buffaloes are slaughtered besides many more sheep and fowl and large quantities of liquor are consumed. The ceremony extends for over three to five days and includes formal reception of the priest who should conduct the *guar*, the rites of invocation at the cremation sites, the invocation of the spirits of the recent dead as well as those of the past dead of the village that had already gone to the permanent abode of the ancestors, the purification baths, the formal bringing of the previously selected slabs from the hill-side to the village, formal request of the new spirits to the old spirits that they may be taken to the permanent abode of the ancestors, taking the slabs from the village to the place of planting, the sacred cooking of the offerings there, formal honouring of the animals to be sacrificed, the planting of the slabs and finally the sacrifice of the animals and general village feasting. In some of these details particularly in the invocation of the spirits new and old and in the oblations and sacrifices, one can notice parallelism between the Saora *guar* and the Āryan *yajña* or sacrifice.

Death and Associated Rituals

Death results in the loss of a living member to the *kulam marangi* (lineage) unit. The dead has to be properly admitted into the ancestral world by observing various rites and he/she has to be worshipped from time to time. Hence death ceremonies are observed very strictly, and are performed elaborately among Saoras. For a person who dies without any suffering after a ripe age, death is considered to be a normal affair. But for others they take it as the malevolent action of spirits. Death is detected by the permanent loss of breath and unconsciousness. The corpse is then placed by the side of pestle in the verandah. To announce the death, Saoras fire *viddia balan* (a rude gun). Death is informed to all the *kulam marangi*s of the other villages by a messenger. All the kinsmen present cry aloud and soon a person is considered to be dead. After all the *kulam marangisi*s gather, the corpse is then given turmeric water bath. Again the corpse is placed on the floor at the pestle and is covered with a cloth. At the time of death water is poured in the mouth and the door opened to allow the soul to leave the body. They don't remove the ornaments. The whole body is coated with oil and turmeric. Around the corpse grains are poured in a row and these grains are to be cooked by the *siggamaran* on the third day after the ashes are collected from the cremated place. Fresh fuel of mango trees is made ready and the corpse is carried by four persons to the *kinthalan* (cremation) ground. *Siggamaran* carries fire. Grains are to be thrown behind the corpse throughout, while carrying it to the cremation ground. *Siggamaran* sets fire to the corpse.

Persons dying with epidemic diseases are buried in a separate burial ground. If a pregnant woman dies they don't remove the embryo out, but her belly is pierced at three places with a knife and is cremated. If they fail to do so it is believed that there will not be rainfall in that area. All the cooked food and even water are thrown away after the death of a person in the village. If the dead body gets delayed in taking to the cremation ground, the other people in the village cook their food under a tree, outside the village. All the persons who attended the cremation return only after the corpse is fully burnt. Take bath at a stream before they return to their houses. The corpse is cremated with ornaments and a few implements. Silver and gold ornaments are removed.

The mourning lasts for three days. During these three days they play *kadingen* (a musical instrument) during nights to frighten away the dead man's spirit so that it will not come back to the house. During these three days it is a taboo for the family members to go for hunting or to do any work.

If a woman dies, she will be taken back to her parents' village and is cermated there. In case the village is at a long distance she can be cremated at her husband's village and the ash and bones will be taken to her parents' village to perform further rites.

There is a considerable influence of Hinduism on the Saoras of Mandasa area. Here they refer to a brāhmaṇa to ascertain whether the time of death is auspicious or not. If it is inauspicious, they leave the house temporarily. The tobo-period which one has to vacate the house will depend upon the degree of inauspiciousness. On the day of re-entering, the house is plastered with cow-dung. The brāhmaṇa comes and burns seven types of sticks, chants hymns, and sprinkles water to mark the end of pollution.

At the time of ceremation all the *kulam marangi* go to the cremation ground. After the corpse is completely burnt, they demarcate around the ash, and on the way seven small vertical lines are drawn and thorny branches are placed. By this, they believe that the ghost cannot come back. After that all go to a stream and a ceremony is performed on their way to the village. The *kudammar* (religious specialist) invokes all gods and ancestors and asks the cause for the death of the person. A fowl and liquor are offered to the spirit who caused death. He appeals to the spirit to be pleased with it and not to do further harm to anybody. Food is prepared by mixing *limma* (*neem*) leaves, and after eating and drinking there, they go to their village. Before entering the house, salt and chilly are placed in fire and a few drops of water are poured on the roof of the house by each person .

The purification ceremony falls on the seventh or twelfth day, which is called *jamane puran*. All the *kulam marangi*s contribute rice and money to this rite and cook in one new pot and a small portion of the cooked food is taken to the cremation ground and is placed on the demarcation made round the ash, and also on the seven vertical lines drawn. At a distance from the cremation ground an oven is made with three rocks and worship is done by offering liquor. A fowl is sacrificed there. A small portion of the food brought by each male lineager will be placed there, and each one says "Here we have given you food and a fowl. So please don't do any harm to us." All of them take bath and cook food with *limma* leaves, and eat together. Then they return to the village after drinking liquor.

Limma is a rite celebrated generally on the third day, when the burial of ashes and bones is done. On this day the food is cooked with *limma* leaves, hence the ceremony is called *limma*. All *kulam marangi*s in particular attend to this. In Seetampeta area, a small miniature hut is constructed there in the cremation ground to make the soul rest there. In the Bhadragiri area, the Saoras erect three to four flags instead of a hut. After this is done a fowl is sacrificed for the dead and also for the ancestors. The food is cooked with *limma* leaves. Eating and drinking thereafter follows.

In all the three areas we visited, *Sikunda* ceremony supersedes *limma* at irregular times, and this postpones the *guar* and *kerja* ceremonies. If a number of persons die in a *kulam marangi* unit this rite is celebrated collectively at a particular house. One day before the *kudammar* followed by instrumental music, they gather all the souls of the dead in a pot by visiting the houses where the death has taken place. A long thread and a ladder are placed over the pestle in the house, touching the roof above and the thread placed in the pot. They believe, the soul enters the pot through the ladder. All the souls of the dead are brought together and the rite is performed in the house where all the *kulam marangi*s attend and offer rice and money for performing the rite. *Kudammar* invokes all the dead persons and offer a buffalo to them. Guns are fired at regular intervals. A small religious rite is also performed at the cremation ground where a buffalo is sacrificed. Under a tree all the *kulam marangi*s cook, eat and drink.

The next elaborate and most expensive rite is *guar*, where honorific sacrifices of buffaloes are made. The *guar* ceremony is more significant and prominent of all rites for the dead. *Guar* ritually means erection of stones (*gu* = to plant, *ar* = a contraction of, *arangen* = a stone). *Guar* is performed after a good harvest year. The souls of all the dead in the *kulam marangi* unit, after the last *guar* ceremony, are included in the company of the dead ancestors, and is liberated from the underworld ceremonially with the performance of a *guar*. The *guar* is performed to enable the souls to rest permanently in an ancestral abode. It is generally believed that the soul remains hungry till the *guar* is performed.

Each *kulam marangi* unit has its own group of menhirs, just as each has its own cremation ground. They are generally outside the village under any tree. If more lineages erect menhirs under the same tree they however, erect them distinctly. The height of the menhirs to be erected is not specified. It is a common practice to erect big stones for the elders and smaller ones for the younger to honour them.

A women after marriage does not change her affiliation with that of her husband's lineage. Hence, after death, in her husband's village when the *guar* ceremony is performed symbolically wooden pole is also erected along with the memorial stones in honour of the dead of the husband's lineage-members. On the other hand, when *guar* is performed by her lineage-members a permanent stone is erected for her.

All the *kulam marangis* have to erect menhirs only at one place. The day of celebration of *guar* is informed to all the *kulam marangis* well in advance. The senior elders of the *kulam marangis* organize the proceedings. All the lineages have to contribute for conducting the *guar*. After ceremonially invoking the dead, the liquor is offered to the dead and at least a buffalo is sacrificed in honour of each dead. Then they erect the memorial stones.

If there is a death in one's sisters house, it is obligatory on the part of the brother to bring a buffalo/goat/fowl and kill it before his sister's house, at the time of conducting a *guar* ceremony for the dead, to express his solidarity. The dead man's friends (*gadi mar*) may also bring an animal, individually, for sacrifice to boost up their friendship.

After the ceremonial erection of the menhirs, the *kulam marangis* participate in an affinal kinship. The guests have a feast; they consume much liquor. The rest of the time is spent in dancing.

Another common ceremony to be performed to the dead is *karja*. Generally to avoid expenses at many places, this is mixed along with *guar* and celebrated at the same time. In this rite also slaughtering of buffaloes is a common feature.

Lijap is the last ceremony which is generally performed after harvest to persuade the ancestors to give good crops in future. It is not a common rite for all the *kulam marangis*, and is performed by the individual families.

The soul of a dead person is believed to cause harm until they perform all the above-mentioned ceremonies.

The different stages in the life-cycle ceremonies, mentioned earlier, like separation, margin and aggregation can be observed together.

Death among Saoras is marked by the observance of pollution by *kulam marangis*. Death itself is identified as a separation of the soul (*rup rup purudan*), located in the heart, from the body. Such a person is called a *kaiyal mar* (a dead person), who passes through a threshold or margin stage before reaching the ancestral world. During this period a number of ceremonies are observed to appease the soul of the deceased. Ultimately, the dead is aggregated into the ancestral world with the celebration of *guar* ceremony and the erection of a menhir. Even after this, the ancestors continue to guide the living *kulam marangi* in several ways. Every year, in the month of May, they celebrate a ritual called *jommolpur* (seed sanctification ceremony). In this ritual, the seeds to be sown/ broadcasted are ritually sanctified by the ancestors. A black goat is offered to them as a token of thanks-giving.

In my recent visit I found many Saoras embracing Christianity to avoid expenses on religious rituals, especially death-rituals. Fortunately, I have observed a *guar*-ritual being celebrated after seven years in the village with less pomp and glory than about thirty years back, i.e., when I was doing fieldwork for my Ph.D. programme. It is appreciating that these rituals have become obsolete in course of time. A video is made on the *guar* by the Dept. of Anthropology, S.V. University recording the event.

References

Elwin, V., 1955, *The Religion of an Indian Tribe*, Oxford University Press, London.

Sitapati, G.V., 1938-43, "The Saoras and their Country," *Journal of the Andhra Historical Research Society*, Rajahmundry.

Suryanarayana, M., 1977, "Marriage, Family and Friendship among the Saoras of Andhra Pradesh," unpublished Ph.D. Thesis submitted to the Andhra University, Waltair.

16

Death
Sociological Interpretation

B.D. Tripathi

How society and death are related to each other? The answer to this question is covered in *Sociology of Death*. Society is affected by the Phenomenon of death in many ways. Similarly, death too is affected by the beliefs and rituals prevalent in a particular society.

How Society is Affected by Death

Death saddens society. Nobody wants to die but death occurs. Death does not discriminate between poor and rich, old and young, man and woman, doctor and patient, sinner and virtuous, ruler and ruled. Death comes to all. Death is the leveller. There is no escape from death. Man has to adjust himself with the inevitability of death. Death is certain; it cannot be avoided. It is said that the day a baby is born, it is awarded a suspended death sentence which is executed later. The phenomenon of death creates despair in man. He is disenchanted from the worldly affairs, the moment he is reminded of death. There are some who see no meaning in raising huge buildings, maintaining huge bank balances as they do not accompany them after death. Even the body which is so close to man is left here as he migrates to the other world. Death-induced disenchantment motivates many for renunciation. People renounce the world and become *sādhus*. The institution of asceticism is the handiwork of death. Buddhism was born from the soil of death. It was death which moved Gautam to develop a new system of religion called Buddhism.

Death does a good thing to society. It reduces the frequency and intensity of conflict among men. Now, how does it do? Keeping death in view, man reviews his actions "Why this mad rush for power and pelf, property and position? Death will one day snatch everything from my possession. So, why should I take so much tension upon my head? Why not live in peace and contentment?" All such ideas related to death hold man in check and reduce tension and conflict in society.

There is huge literature in each society on death. The central theme of such a literature is that life of man on the earth is transitory and fleeting. As such, it is meaningless to enhance worldly possessions. Enhancement of possessions cannot avert the event of death. In fact, such a literature is a gift for society from death.

How death is Affected by Society

Death pre-exists society. Society is not simply the congregation of individuals. Society is born when the congregation of man generates a culture, belief and ritual system and adheres to them. Adherence to different items of culture creates an idea of *we-ness* among the members of the societies concerned. It is this *we-ness* of the adherents which constitutes the foundation of society. Every society, be it tribal, intermediate or modern, stands committed to save its honour. When the honour of a society is at stake, members are expected to save it by sacrificing their lives. Those who fail to do so, become objects of scorn in the eyes of the societies concerned. Social mind weaves literature and myths in which men dying for the honour of their society are glorified.

If a society is fairly integrated, its structure is cohesive. Egoistic suicide is held in check in such a society. In cohesive society, suicide, actuated by personal considerations, is severely condemned. Such a condemnation puts a barrier on the frequency of egoistic suicide. But if a society grows more cohesive, the number of persons ready to lay down their lives for certain causes increases. In such a society, frequency of altruistic suicide grows. Army is an example of highly cohesive society. Here soldiers and fighters do not ask *why* should they sacrifice their lives. They simply *do* as ordered and *die* for the cause.

There are societies which evolve belief-systems wherein persons dying for a social cause are promised heavens where the martyrs enjoy all sorts of pleasure unmixed with pain. In Jainism, death through *prāyopasan* (welcoming death by foregoing food) is glorified. There are sects which openly abet their followers for suicide and the followers do so *en masse*. Centuries back, it was a common belief that those committing suicide in Kāśī attained liberation. So, people from different parts of India came here and committed suicide at Kāśīkarvaṭ near the Viśvanāntha Temple.

In short, sociology of death deals with the interplay between society and death.

17

Death and Social Existence of Man

Hetukar Jha

In the *Mahābhārata*, the famous epic of the Hindus, there is a chapter containing the dialogue between Yakṣa and Yudhiṣṭhira. Yakṣa asked the question: "What is quite surprising in this world?" Yudhiṣṭhira replied that "everybody in this world knows that his/her death is certain. Those who are born are bound to die. Innumerable persons die everyday before the eyes of all and, yet no one is free from the lust for life. Nothing could be more surprising."[1] Yudhiṣṭhira's contention is an eternal truth. Every living being on this earth has a limited span of life. In the famous book, *Yoga Vāśiṣṭha*, Lord Rāma says that man's life has no certainty, it is full of variation and comes to an end abruptly. Death is extremely cruel. However, man nourishes much confidence in his young age and pursues his desires.[2] In this version of Lord Rāma, both death as well as the desire to live are held to be true. Death is definite, but the desire to live also exists in the mind of everybody. The two are contradictory to each other. While Yudhiṣṭhira remained silent regarding the contradiction of life and death, Lord Rāma recognized it well.

In different religious scriptures of Hindus, attempts have been made for resolving this contradiction. However, a few

---

1. *Mahābhārata*, Yakṣa-Yudhiṣṭhira Saṁvād, *trayodaśādhika tṛṣaṭamodhyāya*, śloka 116.
2. See *Yoga Vāśiṣṭha*, vol. I, ed. and tr. into Hindi by Shri Ram Sharma Acharya, Sanskrit Sansthan, Bareli, U.P., 1996, p. 163.

questions regarding death may be relevant to the issue of discussion here. The questions are: *What* is death? *Who* dies — one *who* is living or is the *life* of one who is living that ends? What does one possess which he loses by death? Or, does he lose everything that he has when death comes?

Mahamahim Gopinath Kaviraj contends in this context that Dattatreya's school of thought presents a categorical description of death. According to him, as destiny brings one's end, his five *prāṇas* merge in their respective elemental spheres, his sense-organs lose the power of action and that power lapses into the fold of the unconsciousness. Only *saṁskāra* remains with him and he slips into the realm of the unconscious. He, then, acquires a minute shape. This event is known as death.[3] In different cults different terminologies have been used for describing it. One thing, however, appears to be clear that in Hindu tradition death is not considered to be the end of one's existence. The constituents of the body are supposed to merge in their respective elemental spheres and the soul takes a minute cover. So, if death is supposed to bring an end to somebody, it is the shape or form (not the content) of his/her body that ends. A living person is identified not only with his body but also by his name. With his name his deeds are associated. Besides, it is also believed that he possesses a soul. So, there are broadly three dimensions of a living person's existence, his body, his name and his soul. Death brings an end to only one of the dimensions of his existence, that is the shape of his body. Death comes as the age (*āyu*) of the body expires. The age of the body depends upon destiny (*prārabdha*) or time (*kāla*). The time of the existence of the body is different from the time of the existence of the name of the person. The existence of soul is supposed to be free from the bonds of time. Thus, the different dimensions of the existence of a person have different relations with time. Here, a discussion of what is time may not be out of place.

3. See Mm. Gopinath Kaviraj, "Adi Guru Dattātreya aur Avadhūt Darśana" (in Hindi) in *Bhāratīya Sanskṛti aur Sādhanā* (in Hindi), 1st vol., Bihar Rashtrabhasha Parishad, Patna, 1963, p. 204.

In the *Śaradā Tilaka*, a classic text of Tāntric philosophy, it is said in the context of cosmogony that the moment Lord Śiva realizes the existence of Kālī, the Śakti, in Him, it gets transformed and consciousness emerges in Him and with consciousness, *kāla* or time begins. Emergence of consciousness indicates the emergence of pulsation movement. So long as there is pulsation, there is movement and there is time.[4] In the *Yoga Vāśiṣṭha*, Lord Rāma says that nobody can see time, because time does not have any bodily or physical shape. But, one realizes its existence as he perceives pulsation in living objects and variations of the events of life.[5] So, as pulsation in the body stops, death occurs, that is, its time is over.

The physcial body is considered to be as good as a piece of cloth that is discarded after it becomes too old and useless. New clothes replace the old ones. Similarly, when the body becomes too old, it is discarded by the soul and then it is again born with a new body. Soul is eternal. Lord Kṛṣṇa's maxim in this context, given in the famous text of *Gita*, has been in high circulation in the Hindu world for the last many centuries and people's belief in this context is a social fact. But the existence of soul is beyond the phenomenal world. So, in the present discussion of life and death as perceived in the social universe, consideration of soul as the central dimension of a human being is excluded. Here, only those aspects of an individual's being are dealt with which belong to this world. Such aspects are his physical body, the status of his name and the deeds done in the course of living his life. Both the status of his name and that of his deeds depend upon his *puruṣārtha*.

In Hindu religious order, everybody is supposed to acquire *puruṣārtha*. *Puruṣārtha* has four constituents, namely, *dharma*, *artha*, *kāma* and *mokṣa*. All these aspects have been discussed in detail in the literature of *dharmaśāstra*.

However, here *puruṣārtha* is discussed from the socio-political, that is, existential points of view which were pre-

4. See *ślokas* 5 and 7 of first *paṭala* (chapter).

5. *Yoga Vāśiṣṭha*, *op. cit*, p. 162.

sented by Vidyāpati, a great poet of Maithilī and a great scholar of Hindu polity as well as *dharmaśāstra* in the medieval period (late fourteenth and early fifteenth centuries).[6] A discussion of *puruṣārtha* in socio-political context would, hopefully, help in understanding death as it is understood in the Hindu society.

Before dealing with *puruṣārtha*, Vidyāpati raised a very important question regarding the existence of man in his book *Kīrtilatā*. This question is: "What is the essence of man's existence in society?" Then, he deals with this question and says that man's existence as man depends upon whether he possesses dignity or not. If he/she has dignity, that is, of his/her dignity is recognized by the society, he/she may be supposed to be existing as human being. In absence of dignity, one loses his social existence though he may physically continue to exist.[7] Vidyāpati thus theoretically separated the social existence of man from his physical existence. Martin Buber dealing with the existence of man in the twentieth century considered that for man it is essential what he should be recognized as what he is and also as that he can be in future by others.[8] Buber's view virtually supports Vidyāpati's contention. The former, however, does not say much about how an individual can secure recognition from others. But, Vidyāpati elaborately dealt with how an individual could secure dignity and make his social existence meaningful to him as well as his community.

In this context, Vidyāpati emphasized in his book *Puruṣa Parīkṣā*, written in Sanskrit on *Daṇḍa-Nītī*, that the dignity of man depends upon manliness that he is supposed to possess

6. See Ramanath Jha, ed., *Puruṣa Parīkṣā of Vidyāpati Ṭhākur*, Darbhanga Series 1, Patna University, 1960, p. 16.

7. See V.S. Agrawal, ed., *Mahākavi Vidyāpati Kr̥ta Kīrtilatā* (original text in *Avadhūta* with Hindi translation by the editor), Sahitya Sadan, Jhansi, 1962, pp. 15-16.

8. See Martin Buber, *The Knowledge of Man*, English tr. by M. Friedman and R.G. Smith, George Allen & Unwin Ltd., London, 1965, p. 68.

and acquire. The attributes of manliness, according to him, are courage, sense of discrimination, perseverance, acute wit, exact memory and knowledge. Besides these, he must also acquire *puruṣārtha*. As said before, *puruṣārtha* is constituted by *dharma, artha, kāma* and *mokṣa*. The first three *puruṣārtha*s are related to man's existence in society, the fourth one, *mokṣa*, has nothing to do with one's community. Vidyāpati discussed *dharma, artha* and *kāma puruṣārtha*s elaborately in the *Puruṣa Parīkṣā* and asserted that having consideration for others/ community helps one in achieving *puruṣārtha* in all the aspects of *dharma, artha* and *kāma*.[9] For example, according to him, performance of one's *dharma* requires following simply his *kulācāra* (rites and rituals traditionally associated with his family/lineage) and *sādhāraṇa dharma* (that is, having no desire for other women and other's property and committing violence to none). By following *sādhāraṇa dharma*, one cannot indulge in sexual and economic exploitation of others in society and, at the same time, he cannot indulge in violent activities. Righteousness thus defined directs one to respect other's position and existence in society.[10]

Similarly, in the context of activities related to *artha puruṣārtha*, Vidyāpati says that it is always desirable to work for acquiring wealth by adopting proper means, but, at the same time, one must be *iṣṭaputin*, that is, he should use his property or wealth for his own pleasure and at the same time, he must also use it for the benefit of his community.[11] In this context, it may be said that the practice of giving gift (*dāna*) to others and that of excavating tanks and wells for the use of all the members of the community have a long tradition in our society. Even in the sphere of *kāma puruṣārtha*, Vidyāpati holds that sexual relationship has to be based on love and trust for each other. One must consider the other partner's dignity.[12]

9. See Hetukar Jha, *Man in Indian Tradition: Vidyāpati's discourse on Purush*, Aryan Books International, New Delhi, 2002, pp. 66-101.
10. *Ibid.*
11. *Ibid.*
12. *Ibid.*

Thus, consideration for others and the whole community is crucial to the process of achieving *puruṣārtha*. The achievement of *puruṣārtha* brings *kīrti*, that is, good name to one who achieves it. This good name helps him to acquire dignity and make his life meaningful from the social points of view. In Sanskrit, there is a proverb, *kīrtiryasya sa jīvati*, that is, he lives who has earned a good name. So, his name continues to survive in the community through his deeds even after his body expires. Name is considered important in other societies as well. But, in Hindu society, its importance is quite evident as there is a long tradition of *nāma japa* and *nāma kīrtana* (the practices of repeating the name of the god/goddess hundred times or thousand times and chanting the names of the god or goddess).

In the beginning, the issue of the contradiction of life and death was raised. The religious scriptures of the Hindus generally deal with it in abstract terms imagined and posited in different periods of history. But the way this contradiction is tackled in the socio-religious tradition of the Hindus is far from being abstract. Life and death of a person are not taken to be dichotomous. A man does not live only physically. His social existence is no less important than his physical being. So, his name does not end with the end of his body. Time for the existence of his body may be limited, but the time for the continuity of his name depends upon his *kīrti*, the *puruṣārtha* he has achieved, and, therefore, it is generally much longer than the time of the body. The body-time does not coincide with the name-time. So, one may live even after his death or he may die (if he has lost his dignity) even while he is alive. Life and death are visible phenomena in society, and both may be and are generally observed to be affecting the existence of everybody in the society. The concept of *kāla* (time) is thus fractured in the Hindu social order for affording different scales for life and death for the same person's physical and social existence.

18

Death in Kāśī

Umesh K. Singh

DEATH is the final and most awesome crisis of all human beings. Though death is a personal crisis its socio-cultural dimension is most important. In fact, death is a culturally conditioned phenomenon (Bloch and Parry, 1982; Hertz, 1960). The meaning of death lies in the values and normative structure of the society. It is anchored in the symbolism of the culture to which the individual belongs. Not only the meaning of death but the process of dying, the ceremonies of funeral, the rituals and sacraments after the death are all cultural phenomena (van Gennep, 1960; Kagawa-Singer, 1994). It is a religious belief as an element of culture which governs the concept of death and dying (Blazer and Palmore, 1976; Justice, 1997).

Of the various religious and sectarian dogmas and beliefs, Hinduism stands unique as it has interpreted death in quite different ways. In Hinduism, death is not simply the end of life in a biological sense. It is only a stage in the larger cycle of procreation — regeneration. The Hindu concepts of *karma* and reincarnation make death holy and a transitional phenomenon. It is considered that human beings have to pass through 84 lakh birth-death cycles. The ultimate goal of human beings is to attain *mukti* or *mokṣa*, which signifies liberation from the cycle of birth and death. According to the Hindu scriptures, the liberation from bondage could be achieved through good deeds. But there are sacred rituals and sacred places which can contribute to liberation (Whillier,

1995). Death in sacred places and performance of sacred rituals not only enables conquering of death but also the fear of death is warded off.

Kāśī happens to be the most important sacred space where the meaning of death assumes great philosophical and cultural symbolism (Justice, 1997; Parry, 1994). Kāśī is known as *mukti-dāyinī* and *mokṣa-dāyinī* signifying that the death in Kāśī by itself enables the believer to attain *mokṣa* (Eck, 1983, 1985; Lannoy, 2002; Saraswati, 1975). All the sins of mortal beings are washed away if he or she dies in Kāśī. In Hindu psyche, *Kāśī lābha* (death in Kāśī) is considered to be a heavenly bliss. People prefer to live in Kāśī just to die (Justice, 1997). Awaiting death in Kāśī is considered to be the most purifying act.

In this paper, an attempt has been made to find out the socio-cultural dimensions of death and dying in the sacred city of Kāśī. The major focus of inquiry is to find out the norms, beliefs and behaviour patterns relating to death in the broader canvas of the Hindu religion and philosophy as it is evident in the sacred city of Kāśī.

The data for the present study has been collected through interviews with the inmates residing in old-age homes in the city of Varanasi. Only those persons have been interviewed who were more than 60 years of age and were not involved in active occupational life. In addition to these interviews, field observation of the burning *ghāṭ*s has also been made. A selected number of case history of old-age persons has further been collected. Formal talks with the relatives of old/dying persons have been conducted. Institutional survey of the four selected old-age homes/dying homes has also been undertaken to find out the features of these unique organizations available in the city for old/dying persons.

Institutions for Old Aged Persons

Though the charitable homes for the aged, destitute, lonely and sick persons have become rather a universal phenomenon as a part of social welfare measure, yet in Kāśī, the old-age homes have assumed a new significance. No doubt, it is welfare-orientation which has created old-age homes, but in Kāśī, the religious-orientation is much more dominant. Philanthropists and charitable institutions have established these institutions for the old-age persons who wish to spend the last part of their life in Kāśī and to die in this sacred city (Justice, 1997). In such institutions the old aged persons are provided shelter to live in and facilitate their observance of religious rituals. The inmates of these institutions may be both, either very poor and lonely persons or they may belong to affluent families and have led a successful worldly life. Compelled by the feeling of renunciation and also with the desire to share the cultural and religious ethos of the sacred city, they become inmates of these institutions. Some of the important institutions functioning in the city are as follows:

1. Kashi Mumukshu Bhawan, Assi, Varanasi.
2. Kashi Labh Mukti Bhawan, Misir Pokhra, Varanasi.
3. Ramakrishna Mission Home of Service — Home for the Aged, Luxa, Varanasi
4. Missionaries of Charity — Nirmal Hriday — Home for the Poor and the Destitute, Shivala, Varanasi.

Kashi Mumukshu Bhawan started its services in 1920. This organization is run by a charitable trust named Kashi Mumukshu Bhawan Sabha. This organization provides accommodation to two categories of people. Firstly, to those old-age persons who are outsiders but want to spend their last days in Kāśī. These people on account of their religious intentions are called *Kāśīvāsī*s though they are not natives of the city. And, secondly, to those religious personages who are *sādhus*, *saṁnyāsī*s and mendicants having a desire to pass their last days in Kāśī remaining attached to their ascetic life and observing religious activities in the holy city. There are around 40-50 rooms meant for the old-aged *Kāśīvāsī*s. The institution is situated in the southern part of the city near the confluence of the rivers Assi and Gaṅgā. It offers residential facility to those old-aged persons who have cleared their family obligations and want to practice the value of *vānaprasthāśrama* with a desire to take the benefits of *Kāśī lābha*, as well. The pilgrims are also provided with residential facilities but only for a few days. Rooms are allotted to the old-aged persons on a lifelong basis on payment of the charges prescribed by the Trust.

This institution usually perfers those old-aged persons who are spending a retired life and are not less than 65 years of age. The husband and wife both are allowed to live together if they wish to do so. But in all these cases they must have some or the other family/relative contacts who could be called during their illness or at the time of death. The organization has also strong reservations against religion and caste of its inmates. Only those old-aged persons are permitted to avail the facilities who are Hindus and belong to the upper castes namely brāhmaṇas, kṣatriyas and vaiśyas. The organization arranges regular *pravacana* and *kathā* for the benefits of its inmates. Daily *pūjā* and *āratī*s are also performed in the temple situated inside the campus.

Kashi Labh Mukti Bhawan, established in 1958, is run by the Dalmia Charitable Trust. It caters mostly to the lower middle class and lower class old-aged persons belonging mostly to the eastern parts of Uttar Pradesh and Bihar. In this institution old-aged people are brought at the very fag end of their life to attain the religious benefits of dying in Kāśī. These old-aged persons either have terminal illness or are very old with no hope to survive any longer. They are brought by their family and the family waits for the death and cremation.

This institution has 12 rooms. A small amount of Rs. 2 per day is charged from the inmates/family members provided free. On the death, funeral arrangements are also made available by the organization. Religious programmes of *bhajana* and *akhaṇḍa kīrtana* are performed everyday for the benefits of the inmates.

Ramakrishna Mission Home of Service started its service in Varanasi in 1900. This religious charitable organization is situated in the heart of the city and is very close to the holy river Gaṅgā. Over the years a number of institutional complex has been developed within the beautiful green campus. A 230-bedded hospital is the nodal institution that provides medical and health to the poor, destitute and patients suffering from a variety of diseases. The campus has got a Sadhu Niwas as residence for the dedicated band of medical professionals and social workers who serve the organization in a variety of capacities. It has got a place of worship and religious congregation as well as a book shop/publication centre to promote Mission's literature and messages. But the old-age home situated within the campus, both for the men and women, is the unique organization of its kind in north India. This old-age home is adjacent to the general hospital, which can provide adequate medical help to the old persons in need. Moreover the proximity of river Ganges and holy temples nearby provide additional attraction to the old-aged persons who want to remain in close touch with the religious symbol and sacred spaces. The Home has 40 rooms for men and women in separate buildings.

This institution is a branch-centre of the Ramakrishna Mission, Belur Math, West Bengal, and has several branches in India and abroad. Its Home for the Aged provides both the pay and free facility as well. It provides medical, food and laundry facilities to the inmates and sometimes attendants are also provided. Those inmates who are not very old or sick are given opportunity to render their services to the social and charitable activities of the organization. Admission of those inmates is mostly preferred who have been associated with the Ramakrishna Mission. Otherwise the person's history may be considered as criteria. Widows, unmarried and persons not having any family support are preferred. Seventy per cent of the accommodation is free of any charge whereas for the paid facility no rate is fixed. Charges are made as per the person's wish and/or capacity. Paid facility also has provision for monthly instalments. This institution is more popular among the Beṅgālī community.

Missionaries of Charity's Nirmal Hriday at Varanasi is a branch centre of the mother organization established by Mother Teressa in Calcutta. Away from the hustle and bustle of the city-life, this institution is situated in a narrow lane at riverside. This organization is working in Varanasi for the last 25 years or so and is not exclusively meant for the old-aged persons only. Rather it caters to the poor and destitute persons of all-age groups and does not make any discrimination on the basis of religion, caste and gender. This institution is run on the funds and guidelines of its main centre at Calcutta and is looked after by the nuns recruited by the central organization. It is also aided by the donations and charities of the common people.

Nirmal Hriday serves those people who are destitute, seriously ill, or very poor. These people are brought by the persons of the Missionaries or by social workers. The inmates include those who have none to look after them and are not in a mental and physical state to look after themselves. They are housed in dormitories and provided food and medical facilities by the nuns who are trained paramedics as well. No charge is rendered for the facilities and services provided to the inmates. Moreover the institution provides a two-hour daily tuition to the non-school going local children free of cost.

This organization has the capacity to accommodate approximately 86 persons. It is usually full all the time. Nearly 50 per cent of the inmates belongs to the older categories whereas remaining includes assorted categories of other age groups. The institution does not take children as they are sent to its sister organization situated in the other part of the city. In case of a female, the young women are rarely admitted howsoever precarious their condition may be. The organization follows the Christian spirit of service and honours its inmates' religion. Even on death, the inmates are given funeral according to their religious belief.

Apart from the formal institutional facility available for old-aged persons and the dying persons, in the city, there are a considerable number of old-aged persons who live in rented houses almost as solitary ones. Such persons mainly live near the river Gaṅgā so that they may easily have the benefit of taking bath in the river and performing/participating in religious rituals on the bank of the river. Such persons are often self-supporting, live in rented houses and take the assistance of domestic servants. But there are so many others who are *sādhus*, *saṁnyāsī*s or simply persons with deep religious fervour who live on *ghāṭ*s, temples, *dharmaśālā*s, etc., and without any regular financial support, spend the last phase of their life in Kāśī. Most of these persons are respected by the common man and are supported by gifts — in cash or kind, offering of foods, clothes, etc. Such people thrive on the religiosity of the common man.

Thus, several types of old-aged persons may be seen in Kāśī with the common motive of spending the last phase of their life in Kāśī and waiting for death to liberate them from the cycle of birth and death. These may be categorized as below:

- Educated and affluent old-aged persons living in old-age homes in Kāśī with the spirit of renunciation and desire to attain *mokṣa* in Kāśī.
- Affluent old-aged persons who, without the institutional support, live in Kāśī and wait for death.
- Religious personage of varying degrees who live in Kāśī on the charitable disposition and religiosity of the common man.
- Those old-aged local residents, who either live with their family or living in their house without the presence of family members, the latter having migrated

elsewhere. Such persons live a religious life and wait for the death to come.

- Destitute/poor old persons living in the old-age homes with the care and support of the charitable institutions.
- Those widows who because of the stigma of widowhood in their family/caste live in Kāśī and pass the rest of their life in the sacred city of Kāśī.

Our exploration of the circumstances/reasons which contributed to making the old-aged persons inmates of old-age homes is very significant and presents a distinct picture on the basis of differential institutional setting of the old-age homes in Kāśī. As observed in the Kashi Mumukshu Bhawan and Ramakrishna Mission, the inmates though having varying social background by and large follow a common ideology of death and dying in Kāśī. It may be noted that not all the inmates of old-age homes in Varanasi are socially ostracized persons suffering neglect and care of family members and relatives and have been thrown into the old- age homes because they are just on the verge of death or having no utility in medical treatment. Instead, most of the inmates of old-age homes are there because of individual volition, religious value, renunciation of worldly life and with a keen desire to obtain salvation through death in Kāśī. Most of these inmates are outsiders and have spent large part of their life in congenial familial atmosphere, and in later stage, they have decided to move to Kāśī and spend the last phase of their life in meditation and in performance of religious sacraments.

The respondents of the study have been quite comfortable talking about death, both as a personal happening and as a philosophical construct. For them, death is a natural phenomenon and the acceptance of this makes them fearless about it. The doctrine of *karma* finds manifestation in their belief that it was because of their earlier good *karma* that they are having the opportunity of living in Kāśī, in the vicinity of lord Śiva and the holy Gaṅgā. They, in most cases, had the view that Kāśī is the most suitable place to die because of its religious importance. A small number of the inmates, who were somewhat uncertain about the concept of salvation and role of Kāśī as a facilitator for the same, viewed the city as a place that brings a state of spiritual bliss, solace and peace from the chaos of mundane life's affair; in that way they find the city as a place where they can be at peace while dying. Furthermore the inmates have regarded their sedentary life as a quite engaging one and serving a purpose. They have been of the opinion that their engagement with religious performances and involvement with activities of the old-age home keep them occupied and bring contentment as well.

Some of the inmates have made plans and arrangements for their after-death rituals and have informed their near relatives or the caretaker of the old-age homes about the same. They mainly wish that their cremation and after-death rituals should take place on the river bank of Gaṅgā in Kāśī. Not only that, in some cases they have carefully made financial arrangement for this, so to be sure and not to become a burden after-death. Although in Varanasi there is a government-run electric crematorium, not a single inmate has preference to be cremated there. They strongly prefer the traditional way of cremation, that is, burning the body on pyre-wood. Spending their life as they do in the old-age homes serves a deep psychological purpose by sublimating the peril of impending death. Absorption in religious sacraments, visiting temples, listening to religious discourses, bathing or else performing religious rituals on the banks of the river Gaṅgā have had a therapeutic effect upon the body and the mind of the inmates. Death does not loom large as the curtailment of life but as a continuation of life. The hope of salvation or heavenly bliss by dying in Kāśī adds to the spiritual therapy of the inmates.

In the case of Kashi Labh Mukti Bhawan, the inmates being in terminal stage have lost every control and authority over their personal matters and it is the close relatives attending them who give directions and control over the dying person.

The attendants often remind them of remembering the names of gods and goddesses or helping them in performing some basic rituals connected with the life-cycle of the person who is about to die. In a good number of the cases of Kashi Labh Mukti Bhawan, it was the strong wish of the dying persons that made the relatives bring them to Kāśī so that they could die peacefully and way to their salvation could be paved. It is interesting to note that some of these dying persons had been brought earlier, sometimes twice or thrice, but because of their miraculous recovery they were taken back.

As in most of the cases the visit to Kashi Labh Mukti Bhawan is a terminal visit for the old and dying persons who at this stage may be in coma and/or in delirium. Therefore they may not be aware of their placement in old-age home in Kāśī. However such placement fulfils the familial and social obligations on the part of their family members and relatives. Fulfilment of the wishes of the dying person is considered to be obligatory. The immediate relatives who as a part of this exercise take the ailing person to Kāśī are not only fulfilling the expectations of the dying person but are also contributing to the solidification of social networks and religious obligations. In these cases the relatives of the dying person carry on the religious and cultural traditions. The Hindu society does not leave the dead person all alone but by observing many death sacraments such as *piṇḍa-dāna*, *śrāddha*, etc., to the deceased person leads to formation of close bonds between the dead and the descendents. Institutions like Kashi Labh Mukti Bhawan uphold these religious and cultural traditions.

In the case of Nirmal Hriday, the situation becomes quite different. Here the institutional care and the humanitarian consideration are top priorities. The helpless, the destitute and uncared ones do not have any philosophy of death with them. They simply die, do not bother about how to manage dying and have no thought as to what would happen to them after death. This alienation towards death is part of the experience of their existential situation. To care about such persons on humanitarian consideration does good to the concerned individual. But it contributes much to the upholding of those social and cultural values which regard dying persons as precious to society as the living one. Moreover the strengthening of the human society is anchored in the preservation of socially relevant values such as honouring the death through care and devotion. Even if one may not be surrounded by immediate relatives and dependents yet one should have the opportunity to seek honourable death. Nirmal Hriday paves the way for that.

Caste and Variations in the Observance of Death Rituals

Louis Dumont's (1970) concept of hierarchy is all-pervasive system of values in Hindu social organization. Hierarchy is deeply ingrained in the Hindu psyche. Though it is more visible in the formal structure of caste-hierarchy, yet it has manifested itself in every aspect of social and cultural life of the Hindus. The phenomenon of death and its socio-cultural attributes are permeated with the concept of hierarchy. Not only the caste-hierarchy exemplifies itself in life before death as well as life after death, but it is also connected with the death rituals and sacraments as well as the obligations, the roles and the behaviour of the mourners. The concept of purity and pollution and the ritualistic hierarchy govern the treatment to the dead body and the roles of mourners. At Maṇikarṇikā Ghāṭ, which is the major burning *ghāṭ*, the ritualistic hierarchy is very clearly mentioned. The Charaṇa Pādukā is the most sacred spot of cremation which is available to the affluent persons who belong to high caste. Though in modern times, persons with high political power/ bureaucratic status may enjoy this privilege, low caste people are not only deprived of this sacred spot but also the religious rites performed by the Mahābrahman differ. Moreover the behaviour of the members on the cremation *ghāṭ* differs according to the caste status. The Khaṭīks as mourners on the cremation *ghāṭ* do not exhibit pathos and grief which is demanded on such occasions. Instead, the heavy drinking, beating of drums and dances, which generally occur on the death of old persons — appears to be an event celebrating death. The death procession, the acts related to cremation at the *ghāṭ* and the return of the mourners all exhibit the hierarchy of the caste status and the behaviour concomitant with it.

The play of "homogenization" and "difference" in the context of caste and death rituals is enacted with much vibrancy and resonance at the cremation *ghāṭ*. Death is a great leveller, but it is also an event which produces differentiation in the socio-cultural milieu of the Hindu society. The dead body possesses a caste identification. The death rituals and ceremonies have caste definitions. Such distinctions are religiously ordained and socially sanctioned. Therefore everyone though pursuing the common goal of *mokṣa*, yet the manner in which it is to be obtained is culturally segregated. In Kāśī where the traditional cultural ethos has permeated every walk of life, the death rituals reflect the play of "homogenization" and "difference" in great abundance.

Ghāṭ and Death Rituals

A unique feature of Kāśī is the location of cremation *ghāṭs* on the river banks of Gaṅgā. The Hariścandra Ghāṭ and the Maṇikarṇikā Ghāṭ are the two major cremation spots possessing great antiquity and religious significance. According to the Hindu belief, the salvation is smooth if the corpse is cremated on these *ghāṭs* (Eck, 1883, 1985; Lannoy, 2002; Parry, 1994). Even of those who are cremated elsewhere, their ashes is brought to Kāśī and immersed into the river Gaṅgā and sacraments/rituals are performed on the *ghāṭ* (Parry, 1994).

While in the other places cremation spot is away from the populated area, in Kāśī both the *ghāṭs* are situated almost in the centre of the city. The burning of corpse and the death rituals are performed on the *ghāṭs*; while on other *ghāṭs*, other religious sacraments and the blessings of the mother Gaṅgā is invoked. Thus, the sacredness of the burning *ghāṭ* is not antithetical to the sacredness of *ghāṭ*s on the river Gaṅgā but rather an extension of the same.

Cremation is the most important ritual among the death rituals in Hinduism. This ritual is known as the "sacrament of fire" or as the "last sacrifice" (Parry, 1994). The Hindu scriptures contain rules and regulations in detail prescribed for the procedures of cremation (Filippi, 1996; Pandey, 1969). All the important death rituals are observed carefully under the guidance of priests. Though the major rituals are almost the same with all cremations done at Kāśī, however some minor ones vary on the basis of caste and religion of the deceased and also on the basis of the custom of the family to which he belonged. Assistance of experienced relatives is also sought in this regard.

As the funeral procession reaches the cremation *ghāṭ*, the mourners and relatives accompanying the procession look for a place for the cremation and arrange wood for the pyre. The wood is usually purchased from the shops adjoining the burning *ghāṭ*. Though wood like sandalwood and mango are considered sacred and best for cermation, as these are much expensive, people use some fragments of these wood with the wood which is in their reach, price-wise. A funeral-priest is also contacted to assist in the ritual. The dead body is taken to the river bank and along with the bier its lower half portion is plunged in the water. The dead body is given a bath and the mourners offer a few handfuls of Gaṅgā water onto its face. Meanwhile the chief mourner, usually the eldest son of the deceased, gets his head tonsured and his beard and moustache shaved by the barber at the *ghāṭ*. He then bathes in the Gaṅgā to purify himself to become ready for the performance of cermation.

The wood is arranged to make pyre, *ghī* is generously sprinkled over the pyre to make it pure and for easy burning, and the body is placed on it after untying the bier and loosening the thread tied on toes. Over the body, more wood, some *ghī* and bundle of easily flammable dry stems (*sarpat*) are also placed for easy burning. Ritual of *piṇḍadāna* is performed by the chief mourner with the assistance of the funeral priest. The chief mourner then buys the first fire from the Ḍom and after circumambulating the pyre, lights the pyre at the mouth of the dead body — a ritual known as *mukh-agni*. After the dead body is almost burnt, the chief mourner performs another important ritual called *kapāla-kriyā* in which the skull is cracked open by a bamboo stick. To cool the pyre, water from the revier Gaṅgā is sprinkled on the ash after the dead body is completely burnt, and the ash remains of the undistinguishable bones are washed into the river Gaṅgā. The chief mourner takes the Gaṅgā water in a clay pitcher and throws the pot backward over his left shoulder as the pot gets smashed upon the extinguished embers of the pyre. He then walks away without looking back. Leaving the cremation *ghāṭ*, the chief mourner and other mourners move to the adjacent *ghāṭ* and bathe there, offer the Gaṅgā water through observing *tarpaṇa* and return home.

Apart from the rituals observed at the cremation *ghāṭ*s, at the other *ghāṭ*s, and other rituals like *piṇḍadāna, tarpaṇa, śrāddha,* etc., are performed in the post-cremation days.

All the rituals that are observed at the cremation *ghāṭ* are mystical and complex in nature. They hold deep philosophical meanings, for example, cracking the skull open during cremation is done for the smooth release of "vital breath" (*prāṇa*) and the chief mourner's leaving the cremation ground without looking back at the pyre symbolizes the end of all attachment with the deceased. The performance of *piṇḍadāna* and *śrāddha* is done to enable the departed soul to mitigate the sufferings. It is said that a son gets freed of *pitṛ ṛṇa* through performance of *śrāddha* (Filippi, 1996; Madan, 1987; Parry, 1994).

The ceremonies observed at cremation *ghāṭ* are not only elaborate but are also imbued with the cumulative heritage of the brāhmaṇic tradition. These ceremonies indicate that there are much elaborate activities to be performed in accordance to the age-old scriptures with utmost religious sanctity. The dead body is not simply put on the pyre to be consumed by the fire but the whole ritual follows a religiously ordained way in which the dignity of the disposal of the dead body is very well guarded through the observances of religiously prescribed mode of behaviour, activities and ceremonies. Even the last act is couched in the garb of deep mystical Hindu way of life. The finality reaches to its zenith in the manner in which the dead body is disposed of at the *ghāṭ*.

Conclusion

Death is a fearsome proposition — no one likes to die. However, the cultural training and the social mores make the death an acceptable proposition. Nowhere the acceptance of death is so spontaneous as in the case of Hinduism. There are socio-cultural norms, values and practices which make death an acceptable phenomenon in the most natural way. In fact, Hinduism makes the individual to conquer death. The present life is considered to be only a small part of the total cycle of life and death. Belief in rebirth is firmly rooted in the Hindu psyche. *Mokṣa* is considered to be the ultimate goal. Within this general philosophical outlook, is anchored the idea that some sacred spots are much better for dying. All the *tīrtha*s are considered to be worth contributing for this purpose. However, Kāśī is considered to be the most sacred spot for dying and attaining *mokṣa*. This cultural framework shapes the psychological disposition and behaviour pattern of devout Hindus. People prefer to die in Kāśī because of their religious feelings. Before death, they engage themselves in religious activities — listening to scriputres, bathing in the river Gaṅgā, etc.

Old-age homes in Kāśī provide an abode for the old and dying persons who have strong spiritualistic attraction for the holy city. These homes not only facilitate in the process of dying but provide an atmosphere where one can perform religious activities remaining away from the mundane affairs of the world. Peace, solitude, meditation and opportunity to live among the same sort of old-aged persons are the general attributes of the life in the old-age homes. Moreover, the institutional support in the form of old-age homes discharges manifold functions by providing conducive spiritual atmosphere, adequate health care, essential psychological support and fulfilment of the basic physical needs. All these become facilitators where death becomes not a menacing proposition but a natural process of culmination of life. In those old-age homes where the dying and destitute persons spend their last days, the humanitarian and service orientation triumphs over the miseries of the ailing and helpless persons.

References

Blazer, D. and Palmore, E., 1976, "Religion and ageing in a longitudinal panel," *The Gerontologists*, 16 (1), 82-85.

Bloch, M. and Parry, J.P., 1982, "Introduction: death and the regeneration of life," in M. Bloch and J.P. Parry (eds.), *Death and the Regeneration of Life*, pp. 1-44. Cambridge, Cambridge University Press.

Dumont, L., 1970, *Homo hierarchicus: The Caste System and its Implications*, London, Weidenfield and Nicholson.

Eck, D.L., 1983, *Banaras: City of Light*, London, Routledge and Kegan Paul.

Eck, D.L., 1985, "Banaras: cosmos and paradise in the Hindu imagination," *Contributions to Indian Sociology*, 19 (1), 41-55.

Filippi, G.G., 1996, *Mṛtyu: Concept of Death in Indian Traditions*, New Delhi, D.K. Printworld (P) Ltd.

Hertz, R., 1960, *Death and the Right Hand*, London: Cohen and West.

Justice, C., 1997, *Dying the Good Death: The Pilgrimage to Die in India's Holy City*, Delhi, Sri Satguru Publications.

Kagawa-Singer, M., 1994, "Diverse cultural beliefs and practices about death and dying among elderly," *Gerontology and Geriatrics Education*, 15 (1), 101-16.

Lannoy, R., 2002, *Benaras: A World within a World*, Varanasi, Indica Books.

Madan, T.N., 1987, *Non-renunciation: Themes and Interpretations of Hindu Culture*, New Delhi, Oxford University Press.

Pandey, R., 1969, *Hindu Samskaras: Socio-religious Study of Hindu Sacrament*, 2nd edn., Delhi, Motilal Banarsidass.

Parry, J.P., 1994, *Death in Banaras*, Cambridge, Cambridge University Press.

Saraswati, B., 1975, *Kāśī: Myth and Reality of a Classical Tradition*, Shimla, Indian Institute of Advance Study.

Van Gennep, A., 1960, *Rites of Passage*, Chicago, University of Chicago Press.

Whillier, W., 1995, "Truth, teaching, and tradition," in K. Sivaraman (ed.), *Hindu Spirituality: Vedas through Vedanta*, pp. 40-63, Delhi, Motilal Banarsidass.

List of Contributors

Bettina Bäumer, is a specialist in the field of Tantra and Kashmir Shaivism. Since more than three decades she has made India her second home. She is the Editor of the Bulletin of the Abhishiktananda Society.

Madan Mohan Chaturvedi, was associated with Biochemistry and Molecular Biology Laboratory, Banaras Hindu University for many years. He is now Professor of Zoology at the Delhi University.

Lavina Chaubey, is gynaecological Surgeon at the Indian Railway Cancer Institute (NER), Varanasi.

K.G. Gurumurthy, is a former Professor of Anthropology, Karnataka University, Dharwad.

Helukar Jha, is Professor of Sociology, Patna University, Patna.

Majeed Khan, is an expert on rock Art, associated with the Deputy Ministry of Antiquities and Museums, Kingdom of Saudi Arabia, Riyadh.

K.H.H.V.S.S. Narasimha Murthy, is a specialist in *Āyurveda* and Lecturer in Medical Sciences, Banaras Hindu University.

Onkar Prasad, is an anthropologist and musicologist. He is Professor in Palli Charcha Kendra, Visva Bharati University, Santiniketan.

George Rajmohan, is the Director of Maitri Bhavan, Varanasi.

K.N. Sahay, is a former Professor of Anthropology, Ranchi University, Ranchi.

Baidyanath Saraswati, was Professor of Anthropology at the North-Eastern Hill University, Ranchi University, Visva-Bharati-Santiniketan, a fellow of the Indian Institute of Advanced Study, and UNESCO Professor in Culture and Development at the Indira Gandhi National Centre for the Arts, New Delhi. He is the Founder of the N.K. Bose Memorial Foundation, Varanasi.

Partul Kumar Saraswati, studied Geology at Banaras Hindu University, taught Geology in Kumaun University and was associated with the Oil and National Gas Commission. He is Professor in Earth Sciences at the Indian Institute of Technology, Mumbai.

R.C. Sharma, was Director General of the National Museum at New Delhi and Professor in Bharat Kala Bhawan, Banaras Hindu University. He is Director of Jnana-Pravaha: Centre for Cultural Studies, Varanasi.

Ahmed Sageer Inam Shastri, is Professor in Social Work at the Mahatma Gandhi Kashi Vidyapeeth, Varanasi.

M. Suryanarayana, has been Professor in Anthropology at Sri Venkateshvara University, Tirupati.

L. Tenzin, is Professor and Head of Tibetan Ayurveda at the Central Institute of Higher Tibetan Studies, Sarnath, Varanasi.

Yolotl González Torres, M.A. Sch and Ph.D. in Anthropology, is the Director of the Department of Ethnology and Social Anthropology, National Institute of Anthropology and History of Mexico, Mexico.

B.D. Tripathi, Ph.D., has been Professor of Sociology at the Mahatma Gandhi Kashi Vidyapeetha, Varanasi.

Index